# SPIRITUALLY ALIGNED LEADERSHIP

# SPIRITUALLY ALIGNED LEADERSHIP
## BECOMING **SELF** CENTERED

YVONNE THOMPSON, MA, CHRP

**CHANGE**
Innovators Inc.

Change Innovators Inc.
2151 Portage Avenue
Winnipeg, Manitoba
R3G 0L3
Canada
www.changeinnovators.com

Editors: Lisa Fugard and Lois Weston-Bernstein

Illustrations: Tree of Abundance, by Cory Graham
   Other illustrations by One Plus One Designs

Printed and bound in Canada by Friesens.

First printing

Library and Archives Canada Cataloguing in Publication

Thompson, Yvonne, 1960-, author
     Spiritually aligned leadership : becoming self-centered
/ Yvonne Thompson.

ISBN 978-0-9865893-2-4 (pbk.)

     1. Leadership. 2. Management. 3. Parenting. I. Title.

BF637.L4T46 2014          158'.4          C2014-906364-4

*This book is dedicated to all of the spiritual leaders in the world who dedicate their lives to spreading the message that there is a different way of being in the world. I have been heavily influenced by each of you and believe that the world can never have too many spiritually aligned parents, children, teachers and business leaders. Together we can shift the planet. To my son, Mike, who has become my role model every single day; to my son, Scott, who truly showed me the way and forced me to face my own spiritual alignment; and to my son, Geoff, who continually surprises me in the most grounded and yet most spiritual way of all. To my husband, Bob, who came along for the ride and in the process discovered his own joy, passion and true alignment. Thank you for letting me share in each of your unique journeys and for becoming my teachers in life.*

# CONTENTS

**Part III—The Many Roles of Spiritually Aligned Leadership**

# PREFACE

# WHAT IS SPIRITUALLY ALIGNED LEADERSHIP?

When I describe *Spiritually Aligned Leadership,* people have a tendency to ask a lot of questions. "So is it a philosophy that assists business leaders? This must be a self-help book right?" In the beginning, when discussing the concepts of the book, people were very skeptical about a theory that addressed parenting, business leadership, community leadership and personal leadership in one book. Many would say, "Business is business and parenting is completely separate. You are going to confuse your readers. There is no way you can address all of these topics in one book." However this is exactly what I hope to do.

*Spiritually Aligned Leadership* is about creating positive energy in everything you do and in every area of your life. For example, when a business manager becomes a Spiritually Aligned Leader, they have this incredible ability to lead employees in such a way that employee engagement levels are very high; employees enjoy coming to work and know that their leader will be candid, honest and consistent all of the time. Employees become curious about the concepts around being a Spiritually Aligned Leader, although they don't articulate it this way. As the leader practices the Tools of Intention (see definitions), the employees become intrigued by a leader who stays consistent, balanced and aligned and they are inspired to emulate those qualities. The leader in turn wants to share the tools and concepts, because that is what Spiritually Aligned Leaders do. They want to spread the love, joy and success that are created when you apply all of the concepts.

Spiritually Aligned business leaders organically, and with no fuss or attention, influence others to lead in the same manner. It is very contagious. People who work for these leaders simply want to be around the leader and follow their example. When they too begin the path of Spiritually Aligned Leadership, there is an immediate increase in joy, abundance and balance that manifests in their lives and they, in turn, become the catalyst for others. This is organic influence!

Parents who practice the same leadership principles are parents who have balance, joy and abundance in all areas of their life, but specifically, they have healthy and balanced relationships with their children regardless of the child's age. In fact it was business leaders and employees who had attended our general Creating Positive Energy workshops, who asked us to create one specifically for parents and the parenting role. Parents who have attended this workshop are shocked at the new perspective they gain when they learn the principles of Spiritually Aligned Leadership and practice the tools we provide.

We all play different roles in our lives, but whether you are a parent, teacher, business leader or community figure; the tools we present in this book are universal. Spiritually Aligned Leadership is a way of life that creates positive energy and is a very simple approach to dealing with life's challenges and opportunities.

In the beginning, applying the concepts may feel unsettling and confusing. We will challenge everything you think about when it comes to your relationships and your interactions with the outside world. More importantly, we will challenge what happens in your inside world. As you begin to challenge yourself and practice the Tools of Intention you will begin to shift in the most positive ways. As one of our participants said, "Simple, Impactful and Mind Blowing; Spiritually Aligned Leadership will change your views about yourself and others at your core!"

Sometimes this is a little unnerving and even scary, but we ask that you continue through the book, do all of the exercises and practice the Tools of Intention every moment of every day. You will begin to see the world, and your life in it, through a brand new lens where the glass is always half full, or more likely full to the top and overflowing with joy, abundance, love, peace and balance. Unwanted events in life will cease or reduce dramatically. At minimum, you will get relief, you will have new tools for managing stress and you will be better prepared to move through the unwanted and undesired events of life.

This book is divided into three parts that address all aspects of your life.

Part I, *The Exploration,* provides exercises for identifying where you are right now in your life, what you believe is going well and where your challenges might be. You will explore the "Roommate" in your head and begin to make decisions about what you want in life and what you want to let go of.

Part II, *The Tree of Abundance and Tools of Intention,* provides a visual overview of the Tree of Abundance—a model used to share our philosophy about life and its unique journey. This section provides details for each of the tools and techniques known as the

Tools of Intention. We explore how to integrate each tool into your life for better balance, peace and joy.

Part III, *The Many Roles of Spiritually Aligned Leadership,* is my favorite because I share the significant value that comes from applying the Tools of Intention and Spiritually Aligned Leadership philosophies in each area of our life. We look specifically at parenting, and business leadership as well as those significant relationships we have with our partners and how we can begin to detangle.

## Definitions

I use some language that may be new to you. I have also created little sayings for things that make great sense to me, but may confuse readers. Because of this I have provided some definitions for you in advance. I hope that this assists you when moving through the concepts and materials.

### Tree of Abundance

This is the name we have given to the model we created to provide people with a visual of our philosophy of leadership, life and the desired or undesired events that show up in our lives.

### Tools of Intention

The roots of the tree show all of the tools we practice when becoming a Spiritually Aligned Leader. They outline the practices and beliefs of those who seek relief, balance, peace, joy and abundance in all areas of their life.

## Spiritual Alignment

I intend no religious connotations when I use this term. It is not my intention, in any way, to challenge anyone's religious beliefs. I strongly value diversity and a person's right to choose their own direction in life and this is in fact at the core of this work. I am a huge advocate of following your own truth. I believe the concepts in this book align strongly with most religious beliefs. Spiritual Alignment simply means that a person is in true alignment with himself or herself. Spiritual Alignment is when a person has done the hard work of being honest with himself or herself to the point where they actually know what they want from the inside out, NOT from the outside in.

## Detangle

I know this is not a real word and that I am supposed to use the word *untangle*. However, *untangle* does not express what I feel needs to be expressed and therefore I use the word *detangle*. The detangling of a relationship is an example where this word is used. When we are so intertwined with another person that we can lose ourselves, we need to detangle.

## Roommate/Noise

I will use the term "Roommate" or "Noise" interchangeably. This term refers to the conversations you have in your head with yourself or with your "Roommate". It could also be referred to as Ego and this is discussed in the book. It is the continuous "Noise" we have going on up there.

*Heart-Centered*

Heart-centered is a term I use when a person accesses their intuitive inner voice. The gut-feel that lets a person know they are on the right track. It is when things *feel* right. We often refer to the left-brain as being the portion of the brain that assists us with logical evidence-based thinking, process and structure. While the right-brain assists with creativity, innovation and bigger picture thinking. The heart-center, when properly utilized, lets us know when things *feel* right or *feel* wrong. When we go deep inside and seek our truth, if we listen carefully, our heart-center guides us.

*Organic Influence*

This is a natural result when a person practices the Tools of Intention and becomes a Spiritually Aligned Leader. It occurs over time in a very subtle, but powerful way. If you are a Spiritually Aligned Leader, Parent or Partner others just want to be around you; they want what you have. They want to follow you and to understand what you practice. People are drawn to Spiritually Aligned Leaders because they create positive energy everywhere they go. They do not become unbalanced easily and they self-correct all of the time. They are consistent, fair and completely open to everyone and their views. They have faith in themselves, in others and in the larger world around them. Interactions with others are *always* positive. This doesn't mean they don't have challenges or obstacles in their lives (although they may have fewer), but it is about how they navigate those obstacles that matters. In fact, obstacles are really not obstacles to the Spiritually Aligned Leader, they are opportunities. People witness their balanced and positive approach to adversity and they want to know how the Spiritually Aligned Leader does it. This is *Organic Influence*. It is created with *no* egoic intent, meaning that Ego is not involved; it is simply the way the person is.

### Compelling Purpose

We use the term compelling purpose in the context of organizational life, however, it also applies to individuals. An organization's compelling purpose is different from the traditional mission and vision statement. Most employees we have worked with over the past fifteen years would say that the mission and vision are usually very one-sided; focused only on the customer. In many organizations it is also not lived or practiced, but more of a nice-to-have statement that looks good framed on the wall. A compelling purpose is the reason you are in business. It defines the organization at its core and is fundamental to the alignment of both the organizational community life and individual contributors. It is lived every day and felt by all. For more information on compelling purpose you can reference my first book, *Leadership for a New World, the Organic Approach to Employee Engagement.*

I also reference or use the word "we" frequently because the compelling purpose of Change Innovators Inc. is to work with organizations, teams and individuals to assist them in creating positive energy, peace, balance and abundance in all areas of life. I see everything as a collective "we" because it is not about one person or one person's philosophy, but is about a group of people (community of practice) who are so committed to facilitating change, particularly in the corporate environment, that I always think in terms of the team. At the core of everything we do is a compelling purpose that drives us to make a difference.

Last but by no means least, enjoy! This book is meant as a road map to happiness, freedom, joy and abundance in every role we play within our material world. My goal is to create a world where every person becomes self-centered with clear intentions and desires that are meaningful to them and them alone; a world where judgments are removed and acceptance is the norm. We live in a world of *free will* and my goal is to ensure that every person I come in contact with recognizes his or her inherent right to joy, love and abundance.

# NOTE TO READER

I anticipate and accept that some readers will find parts of the book controversial. I feel strongly that multiple realities truly exist and I value the many different beliefs and opinions. It is these different beliefs, and ways of being in the world, that make earth such a special place. I respect, honour and appreciate differing views; it is in fact what is at the heart of this work. Remaining inclusive and open to all possibilities so that I can learn and grow is my primary focus.

To protect privacy and ensure confidentiality, I have changed the names of some individuals in this book where necessary.

# SPIRITUALLY ALIGNED LEADERSHIP

# PART I
# THE EXPLORATION

# CHAPTER ONE

# WHAT'S YOUR STORY?

Everyone has a story, whether we want to admit it or not. Often our stories are buried deep within our psyche where it is hard to find them. Many years ago, I decided to go on a journey of self-understanding and this journey forced me to uncover my story.

I was born the second youngest into a family with five other siblings. As with most families, my parents had a significant influence on my early years and, if I was to be truly honest, they continue to have an influence as I head into my mid-fifties. My father is a very assertive, confident and determined individual. He has always valued intellect and mental capacity and as a result is extremely well-read. He also believes that to be successful in life you need to be able to speak your mind clearly and concisely in a direct and bold way. These beliefs served my father well for many years as a business leader in the 1960s, 70s and early 80s.

My father set out to ensure that his children would also have the ability to voice their opinions, to debate and firmly stand behind their views. Like many families, we believed that mealtime was an important opportunity to gather and share events of the day. However, on many occasions my dad would begin a discussion and then encourage opposing views to stimulate a family debate.

Unfortunately, it was not your usual casual discussion between family members. It usually turned out to be a heated debate that often had winners and losers. I now believe that most of us engaged in the conversation to prove to our dad that we were well-read, articulate and able to win. I remember being thirteen or fourteen years old and participating in debates regarding the famine in Ethiopia. I'm not sure what I knew about the famine in Ethiopia, but it didn't stop me from rigorously debating my point of view.

I learned some wonderful skills while growing up in this environment, specifically the ability to articulate my point of view in a clear and concise manner. Each one of my siblings, to this day, is a strong communicator. Unfortunately, there are two sides to everything, and one of the shortcomings of my family environment was not learning the important skill of listening. Listening skills were not valued and to the best of my recollection, were never discussed.

My dad's obsession with intellectual capacity permeated into all areas of our life, especially when introducing friends into the family environment. Often my dad's first comments would be around his assessments of how bright or intellectual he thought someone was. As children we internalized this as the measure of success.

So herein lies the first element of my story. As a young child I struggled at school. In those days I was described as being developmentally slow and overactive with the inability to slow down and learn how to read. These days I would be diagnosed with Attention Deficit Disorder. Back then I was the child who fidgeted, who couldn't sit still. As a result, I did not learn how to read until grade three or four, putting me significantly behind my friends and siblings. It was well-known within our family household that I was not the brightest star in the sky. In a family where intellect and the ability to be well-read were highly regarded, I certainly fell well below the accepted standard and I knew it. As an adult, I realize that the intent of my parents or my siblings was not to reinforce my feelings of inadequacy; however, that was the result.

With a high value placed on intellect, there was significant pressure for each child to attend university (though I'm not sure the pressure came directly from my dad). In my family we now have a doctor, a lawyer, an accountant, a successful senior manager and me, the entrepreneur. Each one of us navigated our childhood and family influences in unique and personal ways; however for me, it wasn't without lots of bumps along the way. Going to university straight from high school was not an option for me because I believed I wasn't smart enough or capable of studying at that level. I spent the first three years after graduating high school, traveling and backpacking around the world; coming home only long enough to make enough money for my next journey. I am not sure whether I was running away from the expectations of my parents to go to school or whether I was running to myself. Those years were definitely full of growth and adventure. Sometimes well-meaning parents and family members create unintentional damaging results.

Another personal attribute that was highly valued in our home was physical image and the ability for one to maintain a proper weight. Being very well-read, my dad often believed that he was an expert in everything including health, nutrition and the appropriate body weight based on a person's height and bone structure. I believe that his infatuation with the body weight of other people, in particular his family members, was based on a true caring for our health, but when a parent vocalizes a concern on a regular basis, it can have the opposite effect.

Another key element of my story occurred at the age of twelve, when shortly after going through puberty, I gained a significant amount of weight. No longer lean and athletic, I suddenly found myself outside the parameters of what my father considered a healthy body weight for my height. While being driven to school or before bed I was reminded regularly that being overweight was unhealthy and that I needed to lose weight.

My mother was a good cook and an excellent baker, and on my fifteenth birthday she made me my favorite cake, chocolate layer cake with homemade Dutch Chocolate icing. It was delicious. As on most birthdays she encouraged me to invite friends for dinner. At a small family dinner, that included one of my friends, we celebrated my birthday which concluded with a present beautifully wrapped in pretty paper by my mom. As I unwrapped the paper, I found a small white box. When I opened up the box I found a small scale. At first I wasn't sure what it actually was. Then I opened the card. Inside was a membership to Weight Watchers. I was officially not just stupid, but fat as well.

It would be an understatement to say that my story affected me for many years to come. My limiting beliefs about myself held me back both personally and professionally. It is really important that we do not underestimate or try to bury the impacts of our stories on our professional and personal lives, for it is the burying of the stories that holds us back from evolution, growth and finding joy.

Even with my struggles as a child, my story is relatively benign compared to those of many of my clients and friends who have bravely shared their stories. My upbringing was not abusive nor was it unstable, but nonetheless the effects of our parents' beliefs can have a huge impact on the children they raise. Intent is rarely the issue. If we are to have growth and evolution we have to consider results and not intent.

## Others' Stories

Many years later, while working as a consultant, trainer and coach, I began to fully appreciate the importance of our stories. I realized that exploring our stories through reflection, journaling and storytelling creates enormous growth opportunities for both ourselves and others. The dynamic, evolved and highly influential people I met and worked with all had significant and meaningful stories.

With permission, I share a simple story that was graciously provided to me by one of my participants in a training class several years ago. I share this story because it had a profound impact on me. Through Mark's story, I realized that I was not the only one who had chosen to intentionally take the journey of self-discovery wherever that led.

I met Mark in Vancouver two years ago while teaching a two-day course. Mark was a middle-aged man working for a large company. As a manager and a respected professional, Mark was seeking further professional development. As many courses go, the larger group was divided into smaller breakout groups to work on problem solving. Each group would discuss the topic and then place their ideas on the flipchart. One person from each group would then report their findings back to the larger group. When it came time for Mark's group to share their thoughts with the larger group, Mark stood up and pointed to the first flipchart paper. This flipchart paper was beautifully written in handwriting, but from right to left instead of left to right. The paper needed to be held backwards and up to the light, so that the larger group could read what was written. As soon as Mark completed the first flipchart paper another member of their group stood up and delivered the remaining information on the following flip charts which were written in the usual fashion from left to right.

On the next break I approached Mark and privately asked him if he had dyslexia. Mark looked at me blankly and simply stated, "No, I don't think so, I've never thought about it." Here was a forty-something professional manager who wrote backwards, but had never considered whether or not he had dyslexia. I know this seems strange, but it appeared to me that, with no judgment, Mark simply accepted that he wrote differently than others. I then shared a story with Mark about someone I know who has a rare form of dyslexia, was diagnosed as a child, and who was lucky enough to get into a research group at a renowned university. The research study assisted the participants in understanding that each of them actually had a very special gift that few will ever experience, such as the ability to read a book backwards and upside down and to process information in a creative and innovative way. Simply put, they could see the world through a unique and very special lens. Mark simply listened.

At the beginning of day two of our training session, Mark approached me and asked if he could share his life statement with me. I was a little taken aback, but realized that this was a rare and special opportunity. He handed me a piece of paper that had a nice border around the text, which stated:

*My Life Statement*

*I will live my life free of prejudice and without judgment.*

*I will seek the good in all situations,*
*regardless of how difficult or trying the circumstances.*

*I will focus my energies toward my foundational principles*
*of trust, honesty, sincerity, fairness, compassion, humility,*
*and human dignity.*

*I will hear the laughter of children, I will see their pride*
*in their faces, I will love and nurture them.*

*I will see the blue of the sky, I will hear life in the air,*
*I will feel the wind on my face.*

*I will have hope for the future,*
*learning each day with the openness and willingness to change so I*
*may grow.*

*And I will be thankful.*

Wow, what a nice way to start my day! Unfortunately, Mark and I didn't have much time to discuss when and why he created this beautiful life statement. I asked if I could keep it and he said sure.

Our class finished and the participants dispersed to various airports and vehicles and I have not seen or heard from them since. However, I did receive an e-mail from Mark several weeks later.

*Dear Yvonne,*

*I really enjoyed meeting you and wanted to thank you for asking that particular question; you liberated me by confirming my suspicions, which for me only started a couple of years ago.*

*I can't answer why I never googled dyslexia, it's odd as I am by nature an inquisitive person and I have since corrected that.*

*However, I didn't spend a lot of time in my research as my brain wasn't interested in reading about symptoms and why I couldn't learn, rather it has been snapping with the consequences of that revelation in trying to understand how do I learn.*

*I have little sayings for everything (wonder if that's a coping mechanism) and as I have said many times, because I believe it, "the question is more important than the answer." Your question proves that true. So I want you to appreciate what your question meant to me.*

*On Monday morning after class as I was preparing for the day something rather remarkable happened to me. For about 20 seconds it seems that every rejection, every criticism, every misunderstanding, every internal embarrassment, and every hurt I have experienced because of this "learning disability" was there in front of me in bold glorious color. And as these images played out*

*I sat on the edge of the bed and my body heaved as I sobbed. As the images ran their course so did my sobbing and immediately afterwards I felt giddy, lightheaded, euphoric, it was, in all seriousness, a life altering moment that I shall never forget and all I could think to say was ... holy crap did that just happen.*

*I have a propensity to think positively, so rather than a disability, I have decided from a personal perspective to tell people who listen that; I learn differently than them, I'm not right-brain challenged, and I can learn and understand things others can't and I think that's pretty cool. From a professional standpoint I want to tell employers that performance is compromised by failing to consider what if any, is the percentage of employees who fail to comprehend the message, whatever the subject, regardless of consequences, no matter what the reason. I am going to learn more about literacy risks and training methodologies that help ensure everyone comprehends the message on their terms.*

*I have started to write about this from my earliest memories because I really like those a-ha moments, means you're growing and I sense I'm in store for some wonderful moments. I would have liked to speak with you further but grateful for what we had. Once again thanks for your insight and the courage to ask.*

*Mark*

I am a true believer that storytelling is one of the most powerful tools we all have at our disposal for learning and sharing knowledge with others. Mark's story does not end because I then emailed him and asked if I could use his story in my training. Several weeks passed and I had not heard from Mark. I was sad because I truly believed he had something important to say and I wanted the ability to share it with my audiences and readers. And then, as luck would have it, an email came into my inbox. Mark had more to share with me.

*I am at this point in my personal journey,* he wrote, *because of everything I've experienced, my learning ability no doubt has played a huge role in shaping who I am, but that revelation/acknowledgment has just happened and like everyone I am the sum of all the parts (past) as it were. I believe I have been to that place Maslow described as "self-actualization", I believe one time led me to draft my life statement.*

The "Maslow" Mark refers to is Thomas Maslow, a psychology professor at Brandeis University, Brooklyn College who was famous for the creation of the Hierarchy of Needs Theory that explores how people move from the basic need for food and shelter to needs of actualization and full acceptance. Mark shared with me, through his email, how he had grown up with an abusive alcoholic father and by age fifteen he worked part-time to save enough money to allow him to move out on his sixteenth birthday.

*But there isn't a happy ending to that story. A lot of things occurred over the course of the next couple of years that inevitably led me on my own path of substance abuse. I describe my life at this point as driving down a dead-end street doing 100 miles an hour with 500 feet to go before I hit the proverbial brick wall. If I wasn't already a social outcast I was becoming one and it's at this place in my life when I was completely lost and stumbled on blindly and ignorantly which shaped and impacted the next 10 years of my life sometimes with devastating effects.*

*What I did about that was I joined the military. Why the military? Call it self-preservation, Maslow's basic needs needed to be met—food and shelter. What the military provided me immediately was imposed discipline which is what I needed to save myself. I also got a seven week imposed detox program. At the end of my basic training I was developing self-discipline just as they had planned and trained hundreds of thousands of others, however I still had an abuse problem, which I have since outgrown that dependency and at this point in my life I can say that I am cured. I recall the personal reward I received when I finally realized that I could learn and have been on a journey of self-discovery and self-actualization ever since.*

*Because I have worked in management for the past 15 years I have the need to connect the dots, I think and see big picture and I guess I don't see my story is anything unique....*

*Sincerely,*
*Mark*

Mark's experience can give all of us courage to examine our own personal stories, for they can define who we are for many, many years. Some of us have worked through our stories and created new stories. Some of us continue to be affected by our old stories, while others have never even considered that they have a story. Our stories affect all areas of our lives including our professional and personal relationships, our management styles, our leadership approaches and our roles as a parent and partner.

If you are a parent with adult children you have a great opportunity to explore what your children's stories are. What would they tell you about what they learned while growing up in your house? Have you ever considered asking them what their story is and how it has affected or altered who they are at the core of their being? Storytelling is important to deepening our understanding. Do they have limiting beliefs that developed during childhood or adolescence? It is important to remember that none of this has anything to do with the parents' intent; it has everything to do with perception, and ultimate results.

My last story is about Gabrielle, a beautiful woman in her late 40s who at the time that I met her did not look a day over thirty-five. Over the years I have become very sensitive to my own energy and also to the energy of other people. I sense and feel things I was never able to sense or feel before. Gabrielle was sitting three rows behind where I was sitting, in a large room with approximately sixty people listening to a variety of speakers. I was drawn to her. I have no idea why, but I needed to speak with her and in fact, I needed to ask her a specific question. Not knowing her name, I approached her during the afternoon break of our second day and asked her a simple question, "Do you journal?" She looked at me with a strange expression and answered, "I can't, every time I journal I begin to cry and I cannot stop crying, so I gave it up." I simply said to her, "You must start journaling, keep journaling, journal every day until you have nothing more to write and no tears left."

She then began to tell me her story. She was conceived out of a rape and her mother made sure she knew this every single day of her life. Gabrielle spent the majority of her life on a self-destructive path of personal abuse and condemnation, believing she was a horrible human being; ugly, unworthy of love, relationships or health. As I got to know her better, I realized she was a beautiful woman who had clearly been on a journey of personal exploration and who had long since learned to forgive and to accept, knowing that none of it actually had anything to do with her. She was simply born into a horrible situation, and as you probably have suspected she is now instrumental in helping others who are in similar situations. This is an example of what can happen when you choose to understand your story and go on the journey. I have stayed in touch with this lovely lady and am glad to say that she continues to explore her story and is back journaling as a method of exploration, healing and is developing a new story.

So what's your story? Everyone has one! You may have long since worked through your limiting beliefs and the old story that you told yourself, but if you are like most people there are elements of your story that still impact your day-to-day life as a leader, partner and parent. Understanding our stories is a critical step in moving toward the journey of Spiritually Aligned Leadership. It is the basis of our first step to finding true alignment.

Get a piece of paper, a notebook or a beautiful journal and write out your story, whatever you can think of that may have helped define who you believed you were in the early years of your adult life. Once you've done that, ask yourself some simple questions. Do I still believe this story about myself? Do these beliefs limit my ability to find true fulfillment and joy? Do these beliefs limit my self-worth? Is this story true? Was this story ever true? Consider any other questions that you think are valuable as you explore your story.

Working with clients, I have discovered that journaling is one of the hardest things for most people to do. In one particular situation, a coaching client purchased a beautiful journal. She reported each time we met that she had purchased it and it had never left her side. She carried it in her bag everywhere she went. However, she would conclude by saying, "But I haven't written anything in it yet." This was the conversation for months. I simply said, "That's okay; when you are ready you will know and you will write in your journal. Just keep it with you." People struggle with journaling because the moment they put something on paper it becomes real; it must be faced, it must be acknowledged. When a person actually begins to journal, they gain some clarity, acceptance of their story and they begin to move away from the old to the creation of a new story. I am happy to say that my client did start journaling and found the practice to be one of the most important tools to understanding herself and where her story came from.

The reason it is so important is that, for many of us, the story was never actually based in truth. It was never reality. It was simply a condition of our environment. I was never stupid nor was I ever an unhealthy weight. I was smart, I was beautiful and I was healthy. But for many years the beliefs that I was stupid, ugly and fat held me back from finding my true self and establishing personal alignment. The beliefs about intellect and healthy body weight were the beliefs of my father, they were not mine, but they were certainly imposed upon me. It was never my parents' intention to have a negative impact on my self-worth and confidence, but remember it is not about intent it is about results.

In our Creating Positive Energy—Parenting classes, we encourage parents to consider how their children perceive what they say and do. In other words, we must consider how the information is received and internalized. Parents often tell us that they only want the best for their children; the problem is they assume they know what is best for their children, when in fact they have no idea. They know what is best from their perspective, but how does this relate to their unique individual children? This is also true for managers and business leaders. Do they really know what is best for their employees? The key is to be sensitive as to how information is received and internalized by stakeholders whether those stakeholders are employees, colleagues or your children. It has nothing to do with your intention. You must put yourself in their shoes every time. Or better yet, ask them in a sincere and authentic way to share with you what it is like to be in their shoes and to see the world from their perspective. This applies to both your children and your employees. You might be surprised at what you hear and learn about a situation, a person or a business environment.

Several years ago, I asked my adult children what it was like to be raised in our family and to live with their father and me. These discussions were some of the most profound conversations I've ever had with my children. They were also the most enlightening and helpful in understanding the role that we played in creating their stories. These discussions were not easy. As I watch my children at the ages of twenty-nine, twenty-eight and twenty-six unravel their stories and find their true self, I am always amazed at how far ahead of the game they truly are.

Once you have begun to tell your story and to open up to journaling and the exploration of how you define yourself, you can ask yourself the next question, "Is or was my story ever true?" I ask you to consider whether your story is true for very specific reasons. For many of us the story is not based on truth, but based on our perceptions and thoughts. For example, when I left home at the age of eighteen, I was slightly overweight, but my limiting beliefs about myself (the thoughts in my head) led me down a path of believing I was fat and the result was that I overate for several years. I also was affected by the fact that I didn't believe I could be successful at university, and so for many years I avoided formal education. The truth was that when I left home at eighteen, I was not an unhealthy weight nor was I stupid, but because I believed I was, and the thoughts I regularly had about myself confirmed this, I was instrumental in creating those exact results. It is very clear to me now that what we think about has a profound effect on our outcomes.

My journey of self-awareness and the strong desire to find my personal truth and let go of my limiting beliefs, began many years ago after a Sunday morning conversation with my husband. In my late 20s, during a traditional breakfast, my husband asked me this exact question, "How come every time we invite people over on a Saturday night, you make a really nice meal, and we serve good wine, but then you proceed to start a discussion, which you turn into an argument and eventually you tell everyone at the table that they are stupid?" I was shocked and in disbelief, but as I thought about the question he had asked, I clearly knew the answer and I made a decision that day that it would never happen again. I would learn to listen and to care about the views of other people and to truly accept that my view was simply my view and no one else's.

I make it sound easy, but it was absolutely not. It was twenty more years of hard work, derailment and reflection, before I began to feel like I was truly making consistent progress. I was letting go of my old story. I had gone back to school, was taking care of my body and was learning to truly listen and value what others had to say. It took almost 20 years to acquire the negative behaviors, so it is not surprising that it took so many to lose them.

The ability to create a new story begins by being honest about the old story and its impact on your thoughts. I had huge limiting beliefs about myself that were based on nothing other than my internal thoughts, and my thoughts were based on things I was led to believe were true as a young person. The only way to find your true self is to let go of the old story, especially if your story is one that does not serve you well or enhance your life. I have found that creating a brand-new story has been a ton of fun. It has opened up doors that I never thought would open and has allowed me to see the world from a completely new perspective.

If your story is one filled with joy and abundance, self-confidence and self-worth, then you are one of the lucky ones. If not, it is time to be honest, evaluate your limiting beliefs about yourself, seek the truth about where those beliefs came from and let them go. As you journey into your old story you must ask the hard questions: Do I know for sure it is true? What is it based on? Does it bring me value? Does it move me forward or hold me back? Does it make me happy? And finally, do I want to create a new story?

In subsequent chapters we will explore our thoughts about ourselves further, and how to begin to shed those thoughts that don't serve us well. We will do some evaluation and reflections on our approach to life, leadership and personal and professional fulfillment. Then we will begin to move to transformation and the *Tools of Intention*.

# CHAPTER TWO

# FEAR AND STRESS

Everyone is affected by fear and stress at some point in their lives. It is important to recognize that fear and stress are uniquely connected and it is difficult to discuss one without the other. Consider how much fear impacts your life. When was the last time you made a decision that at the core was based on fear? Or conversely when was the last time you did not make a decision because of fear? I would suggest that most of us are impacted by fear more than we are willing to recognize or admit. Often our stress is a result of our fear. It is crucial to evaluate the level of fear within our lives; to identify where it comes from, to evaluate the overall impact and to determine whether that impact is positive or negative. Finally, we need to ask, what is the connection between my fears and my stress?

Before we get into these questions I want you to take a moment, sit quietly, and imagine what your life would be like if you had no fear, whatsoever. I don't mean the simple recognition of when it is safe to cross the street. I mean the fear that impacts life's important decisions. What would you be able to accomplish if you had no fear and truly believed that everything you decided to do, every decision you made, would work out exactly as it should and you would be okay with it? How would your life transform if you caught yourself when fear tried to sneak in, and didn't allow fear to impact your choices and your decisions? It is an empowering moment when you realize that nothing can hurt you. For most people this is a profound concept that makes one think of a life of bliss, peace, and reassurance that everything will be as it should be, However most people do not believe that this is possible. I know it is possible and it does result in a balanced, blissful and heart-centered approach to everything. To get there we must become Spiritually Aligned.

**Is Fear Holding Me Back?**

Have you ever met anyone or worked with anyone who always saw the glass as being half-empty and analyzed every situation over and over with a list of "what ifs." I am not suggesting that we shouldn't look at the pros and cons of a decision, but it is critical that we evaluate what underpins the "what if" scenarios. Is it fear that lies underneath? If we go down our list of why we should or should not do something, we need to consider how much fear plays a role. We should also consider how much past experience or possible future outcomes are influencing the list. Often my clients will say, "I am simply being realistic and practical." This may be true however there often appears to be some fundamental information and criteria missing from our decision-making process.

Let's take the typical current business model and corporate environment and consider the decision-making processes used, or more importantly the decision-making processes that are valued. Over the past hundred years, businesses have focused on and valued left-brain activity. We have valued process, efficiencies, technical information, and hard facts including research and data.

We have not valued, to the same extent, our intuition and our gut-feel or heart-centered decision-making skills. As employees and leaders we have been trained to dial down our right-brain activity and dial-up our left-brain activity. Many organizations are rigid in their decision-making models that only include left-brain approaches and, for some of you, the concept of using right-brain, intuition and gut-feel within a business context seems extremely foreign.

The logic is that if we follow, exclusively, what the data tells us, we can mitigate risk and make better decisions. We see the facts as known and tangible. At the heart of many businesses are people who are risk averse and influenced by fear. The challenge with this approach is that the world is extremely dynamic, changing at every moment and heavily influenced by uncontrollable events, people's emotions and an unpredictable global environment. I would never suggest that we should stop using a left-brain approach to decision-making, but it is critical that in today's environment we begin to value, utilize and dial up our right-brain abilities. In most business contexts the skills of intuition, gut-feel, and heart-centered alignment are severely undervalued or in some cases, non-existent. As a result, we often find ourselves heavily regulated, burdened by massive rulebooks with a spreadsheet or Gantt chart at the center of everything we do. This structured and rigid process excludes a significant part of who we are as employees, leaders and basic human beings. We are, after all, heart-centered and intuitive as well as analytical and process oriented. Why not use all of our powers?

One of the most significant negative impacts of our current business environment, built exclusively on left-brain activities, is that we have learned it is better not to be fully honest at work. Business continues to be plagued with subtle deceits and a lack of candidness. Even when our heart-center speaks to us or our intuition tells us something we often ignore it, choosing *to go along to get along*. We avoid sharing our heart-centered message for fear that it will not be valued or appreciated. I am sure you can remember a time as a leader when you intuitively knew what the right thing to do in a specific situation was, but you ignored it, choosing to support the evidence-based information. Individual human beings are also affected by this issue as we have been living in a world where tapping into our intuition and heart-felt gut-feel is not valued. As a result we tend to mislead others and ourselves.

Another challenge, in more recent years, with this very old corporate environment, is that our newest employees, the younger generation, are significantly more intuitive and value the right-brain activities, which by the way, they excel at. They value freedom, autonomy, creativity, innovation and their ability to tap in intuitively. Heavily structured environments with massive rulebooks tend to stifle this generation and hinder them from being highly effective. It also makes it difficult for corporations who apply the 100-year-old business model to attract this significant new talent pool.

If we compare the corporate environment to the new entrepreneurial environment, we see significant differences. Traditional management tends to be risk-adverse, focusing on a left-brain approach, while entrepreneurs welcome a creative energy that is innovative and highly intuitive. We often see small entrepreneurial businesses equally appreciating both left and right-brain abilities and utilizing gut-feel and heart-centered decision-making far more than their corporate counterparts. Most of us would agree, it is more likely that fear underlies decision-making in the corporate environment than in an entrepreneurial environment. Entrepreneurs, especially young entrepreneurs, have just as much at risk, and yet they don't have the same level of fear. Entrepreneurship embraces risk—is built on risk. This is why many young people are looking for ways to stay independent of large organizations as they are not attracted to the rigid fear-based philosophies.

For most of us, fear has played a role in our lives for many years. The level of fear varies with each person, but regardless, fear has an impact. We all know someone who is dreadfully afraid that they will not have enough money. They believe they may never be able to retire and hoard away every nickel, and even then they are not convinced. My mom and dad were extremely cautious about how they spent their money. Up until the day my mother died, she shopped at the used clothing store. I will never know whether this was based on a fear of not having enough, possibly as a result of living through the depression, or whether she felt she did not deserve new things. Nonetheless, they always had significantly more money than they needed or would ever use. Oddly enough I grew up believing that we were poor, when in fact nothing could have been further from the truth. We live in an abundant world where there are numerous choices and opportunities and yet many people cling to beliefs around lack and scarcity.

I have a very dear friend who lives in a small town in Manitoba. She has made most of her adult decisions from the perspective of fear and lack. She believes that if something bad could happen it most probably will. I have watched in amazement for many years how her decision-making has been impacted by her fears. She purchased a beautiful home in a peaceful community about twenty years ago where she proceeded to raise a family and become an avid gardener. She is a professional and one would assume that a solid and consistent income would result in a comfortable standard of living for her. However she has always talked about not having enough money for retirement and fretted that she would have to keep working. Approximately ten years after purchasing her home, which by this time was mortgage free, the community was offered a large manufacturing facility, which included hundreds of new jobs. The plant was built not far from her home. Slowly but surely the neighborhood began to change. Zoning requirements were overlooked and single-family dwellings were turned into multiple family dwellings; neighbors were selling their homes to developers. My friend continually spoke about the impact of these changes on her beautiful neighborhood and also expressed great fear about moving. Questions like, "Where would we live and would we like it as much as the house we have now? Could we even afford to move?" kept coming up. Over a ten year period this was a continual conversation between us. Her inability to make a decision and move on, because of her fears of the unknown, left her unhappy and overwhelmed with the changing demographic of her neighborhood. Eventually the decision was made to move, but by then her house had significantly depreciated in value. The negative thoughts and fears around this situation brought absolutely no value to her and over the years created stress.

At one of my workshops last year a participant shared with me the definition of fear, which I thought, was insightful and fun.

F= False

E- Evidence

A= Appearing

R= Real

What are our fears based on? Usually they are based on information that is not real or at best is extremely old. They are based on stories we tell ourselves about what might happen if we do something or if we don't do something. We create fears based on possible future results or on old past patterns. We need to start monitoring how we feel and what our heart-center is telling us about the situation. Ignoring our intuition and gut-feel about a situation means we have ignored what is vitally important to us. Again we have learned to underplay the value of this internal system and we don't trust ourselves to go inside and ask the hard question, What feels right? In the example above, my friend's feelings, her internal guidance system, had been telling her for years to move and let go of the house she was holding on to, but she was not listening to that system and she allowed her fear to hold her back. A heart-centered approach is very different from a cerebral left-brain thinking model.

I have worked with hundreds of clients who have been affected by fear every day when making decisions. Some clients find themselves extremely unhappy within their work environment, or the positions they have and yet they stay, ignoring their internal voice or intuition that it is time for a change, all because of fear of what might happen if they leave the perceived stability of their job. We are not suggesting that people make quick, rash decisions to significantly change their lives. However to stay in an unhappy and unfulfilling role for years has significant negative impact physically, mentally and emotionally.

Before we move on to examine how stress plays a role in our lives and how it connects to our fears, it is important that we evaluate the extent fear impacts our lives and the important decisions that we make along the way. Get out your journal and over the coming days ask yourself the following questions and when answering, be brutally honest.

► On a scale of one to ten how much does fear impact my life?

▶ When was the last time I made a decision where fear was a primary factor?

▶ Have I ever made a bad decision where fear was a factor?

▶ Does fear hold me back from having and doing what I want?

▶ What would life be like if I had no fear; what criteria would you use when making important decisions if fear had no influence?

Your ability to be honest with yourself when answering these questions is critically important and forms the foundation of your journey to becoming a Spiritually Aligned Leader.

## Always Be Honest Before Kind

*Always be honest before kind* is a fundamental principle that we all need to live by when interacting with our employer and colleagues, family members, partners and in the community. It is taught and practiced in all of our leadership courses and programming. Our clients learn to truly value honesty in its truest form.

Most of us subconsciously avoid being honest with ourselves. We tell ourselves little white lies over and over again. Why? I believe that most of us are unwilling to truly be honest with ourselves because once we start being honest we have to face our fears. We have to make new choices and listen to our intuition and heart-center. We cannot truly be honest with others until we hold ourselves accountable for being honest with ourselves first.

If you think about it, every time you have not been honest with someone, (meaning you don't tell them and yourself the real truth about how you feel on a subject or in a situation) it results in some form of resentment or negative energy and later misunderstanding. There are no cases, that I am aware of, where a person has felt one way, acted or reacted another way, and ended up happy with the results. Over time the individual can feel misunderstood, resentful, or frustrated; all because they did or said something to be kind instead of truly being honest about how they felt on a topic, situation or relationship.

When we are not honest, in an effort to be kind, we hurt ourselves and the other person as well. Here is another way we can look at this concept.

## HONESTY with GOOD INTENTION = KINDNESS

Monitoring intention is another fundamental concept of Spiritually Aligned Leadership and when you combine positive intention with honesty you can never go wrong. Truly monitoring intention is critical and requires honesty, because if your intention is to make the other person wrong or to convince them that you are right, then your intention is not positive. However, if your intention is to improve understanding and communication or to assist another person in considering a different perspective, then your intention is positive. We will discuss intention and honesty in future chapters, but for now your ability to be honest about how fear plays a role in your life is fundamental. Along with this is your ability to ask the hard question: Why does fear play the role that it does and how does it hold me back?

Here is a simple example where honesty before kindness played a significant role in my life and that of my husband's. Many years ago we purchased a piece of property on a beautiful island on the west coast of British Columbia, Canada with the intention of building a home there once my husband retired. When the time came for Bob to retire, we continued to dream about living close to the ocean and building a simple home amongst the huge cedar trees on our property.

We began talking to builders and looking at plans. This went on for months. We finally agreed on a home design and had several meetings with a specific builder. Our plan was that I would continue to work, as my work is my passion, and I would commute back and forth from central Canada. My clients are spread across Western Canada so this would work well. I planned on being at our new home one week of each month and the rest of the time I would travel back and forth from my office in central Canada.

The negotiations with the builder continued and the closer we got to finalizing the details, the more my heart-center (through my tummy) was saying, *Do you really want to build a house? Is this really something you want to do?* The closer we got to signing the contracts, the more I doubted my desire to build a home. Remember, this had been a dream for over ten years; we were about to move forward and I was having second thoughts. Actually I was having an important gut-feel moment that was telling me to stop right now.

How could I tell my husband that I didn't want to build a home? I was committed to living on the west coast and to commuting, but I felt that building a home was too much work, very expensive and would be difficult for both of us due to the amount of time we would be apart.

My big concern was Bob. How much did he want to build this home? Would he be upset and disappointed when I expressed my gut feelings? Two days before we were to sign the contracts and courier them back to the builder I finally said, "Bob I don't want to build a home." In my efforts to make Bob happy and fulfill a ten year dream, I was about to commit to something I absolutely felt was a mistake. Guess what? Bob felt the same way, but didn't know how to tell me. This was an example where *kindness before honesty* could have resulted in a wrong decision for both of us. This happens more often than most of us would like to admit. I think we all share similar stories of trying to make family, partners and our children happy instead of being honest about how we truly feel.

### Stress is Killing Me

As events happen in our outside world, the mind interprets those events and internalizes and often embellishes them. We tell a story about the event, layering in our fears and past experiences. The confrontation with the manager in your company is colored and informed by an event from your childhood or a recent moment of contention with a family member. The stresses from the work environment play out at home and vice versa. And then what happens to a person if both of these environments are unhealthy at the same time?

Our stories usually include some form of fear around what might happen or what is perceived as possible—the "what ifs" start running through our head.

Unfortunately, as human beings we are still afflicted by the primal response to these negative environments and situations.

Emotions of fear or anger arise and then the *fight or flight* reaction takes over. This reaction creates stress in the body. It is important to remember that stress starts in the mind, with our thoughts about the situation or environment, which creates a response in the body. This reaction in the body affects many of our biological systems; most importantly the secretion of additional hormones. In flight or fight situations the adrenal gland produces and secretes additional hormones such as cortisol. These hormones fuel the body with additional energy which most of us feel as an increase in nervous tension or a heightened reaction to things.

In small amounts and over short periods of time, this is not necessarily a negative thing. In fact, this heightened energy level (increase in hormones like cortisol) can sometimes produce positive outcomes. We often refer to this as positive stress; the stress that puts us on our game and assists us at performing at higher levels. But what happens when this heightened stress increases and becomes prolonged? Significant amounts of additional hormones are produced creating adrenal imbalances that have people walking around highly stressed and overly reactive or, in the case of an introverted person, excessively withdrawn. This is when we begin to see the negative effects of stress. For many of us, our sleep patterns become affected, we eat and drink more of the wrong things, and the negative conversations in our heads increase. As the negative conversations continue and heighten in intensity, the cycle continues with additional hormone production resulting in increased stress. It all starts with, *what we think about!* Before we take a closer look at how we can take control of our stress, let's complete a simple questionnaire that helps each of us to consider what is really going on.

**What is Stressing YOU Out?**

Consider, reflect and document the following:

1. What stresses me out? (e.g. My father stresses me out…)

2. What are my trigger points? (When he asks me how much I weigh.)

3. What are my body signals? How does my body tell me that I am under stress?

4. Overall, how do I feel when I am under stress? Consider sleeping habits, eating habits?

During full-day workshops, I often have clients respond, saying, "What isn't stressing me out?" Unfortunately we are living in a world that is perceived as being very stressful, unpredictable and often overwhelming. Again, here is a chance to be really honest with yourself. Remember honesty before kindness. Be true to yourself, no sugar coating it, be candid and recognize that change can only come with honesty.

As you look at your answers to the above questions, consider if what stresses you out *actually* has anything to do with you? I know this seems to be a strange question to ask, but I ask it for a very specific reason. Let's say your answer was "My mother-in-law and how she treats me." Consider what that really has to do with you? If your boss is a controlling micro manager, what does it really have to do with you? You are not incompetent—he/she is a micro-manager. I know what you are thinking: *It has everything to do with me because it affects me.* Herein lies the issue; it affects you because you internalize the situation and because of what you do with the information once it has been internalized. We might add in some fear or negative thoughts toward the person or situation. All of this creates stress. The common denominator is the fact that each of us internalizes our outside world. We bring the outside world and our situations into our thoughts and then we add to it to create our stress.

This is often where people in my workshops want to get up and leave. I get it…it is tough. This is not easy. I have been in several situations where the stories I created in my mind with some basic information resulted in months of stress, unhappiness and fear.

Many years ago, I worked for a large multi-national company. This was my dream job—Branch Manager, tons of autonomy, great group of people to work with and I was really making a difference. I had been there about three years when all of a sudden I got fired. Fired in a nasty kind of way—asked to pack up my things, empty my desk, walk to my car, while they watched me load up and drive away. Back then there were very few rules around this practice and this type of conduct was not uncommon. I hadn't done anything specifically wrong and was given a nice package, but I was devastated. I had always been promoted, head-hunted and sought after, and here I was walking out the door. *It took my breath away.*

It is hard to describe the thoughts that went through my head, but what I can tell you is that for the next six months, I was a train wreck. When I look back now it was the largest pity party a person could have. I created negative thoughts about the people and the situation, which haunted my every waking moment. I had trouble sleeping, my best friend was a bag of chips and cold beer and my overall ability to function appropriately with my kids and family was strained most of the time. Here was an *unplanned, unwanted* event that landed on my lap and I had no choice but to deal with it. I believed thoughts such as, I *wasn't wanted; I'd been discarded and tossed away.* I was unable to successfully participate in interviews for future work, as my negative outlook tainted everything. This was not my finest moment.

I look back now and I know that I "created" a hugely negative and detrimental environment for my family and myself. It took me years to come to terms with the role that I played in that incident and the responsibility I had to take for being fired. It was probably two years later before I began to be honest with myself. I look back now and know that it was one of the most important events in my life. This single event had significant positive impact on me and I would not trade it for anything.

You might be wondering what actually happened and why I got fired. It is really simple; *Ego* got in my way. As mentioned in the previous chapter, I knew how to win a debate, I knew how to hold my ground. I had simply been asked to do something, by my boss, which I absolutely disagreed with. It was something that I fundamentally felt was wrong and I would not back down. In one specific conversation, my boss/supervisor asked me several times to reconsider and in fact he even warned me that if I didn't reconsider he would have to take different action. My arrogance, pride and Ego did not allow me to remember that conversation until several years later. I was too busy creating negative conversations with myself about the whole thing and believing that I had been truly wronged. At the same time I doubted myself and my confidence was shattered. Both of these processes are Ego-based and the conversations in my head, with myself, were debilitating. Herein lies the truth; this event was one of the most important events, created by me, for me, and supplied by the universe as a way of waking me up to say; *this is not what you are supposed to be doing and to get where you need to be, you need to lose that Ego, shift perspective and create something new.* Spiritually Aligned Leaders know that everything happens for a reason and that major roadblocks are placed in our path for an important reason. (More on this later.)

Our ability to look back and connect the dots allows us to see a totally different picture. I wasn't supposed to work at that job for a long time. I was supposed to go out on my own and begin consulting and coaching with leaders; I was supposed to start my own business. Many years later I am able to be truly honest with myself and evaluate that situation more clearly. Nothing is a random event; everything happens for a reason.

I think most people have experienced unwanted, undesired events which, in hindsight, they realize were of value and importance. But what if we could seek the value and the importance the moment the event happens. What if we could ask ourselves: Why is this happening? What can I learn from this event? Why did I attract this event into my life and what is the opportunity? In every perceived unwanted or undesired event there is a huge opportunity; we simply have to look for it. This is not an easy skill to learn or to apply, but it is absolutely possible and as we uncover the tools of Spiritually Aligned Leadership you will learn to do exactly that; look for the opportunity around every event, situation and internal feeling.

If I had been able to look at this event differently, as a Spiritually Aligned Leader would, I could have moved through it faster, easier, and more effectively; learning quickly; seeking the opportunity and acting on that opportunity. We do not have to suffer to learn, we do not have to go through significant trauma when an unwanted event happens. We simply have to ask the *right* questions and then be really honest with ourselves. We need to seek the opportunity and look for the reasons why we attracted the event in the first place. I think everyone experiences events like this which really impact us at the time, but only later do we recognize them as gifts.

It is time to get out your journal and reflect. What is your event? What do you call it? What were the details and how did it affect you in the short-term and in the long-term? Remember that you have both personal and professional examples. Everything is connected. What happens to us in our personal life affects our professional life and vice versa. As human beings we bring our unique selves to every situation. Whether the example is from our long-term past, such as when we were a child or the more recent past, it impacts our working lives. If we want to be the best leaders for ourselves, our families and our employers we have to be honest about this. Our professional life dramatically affects our personal lives and many of us have experienced what happens at home when things are not going well at work.

**Considering A Situation or Event**

An event or situation in my life that did not go as I would have liked. (Give it a Name, you know what it was)

What were your thoughts at the moment it happened (while it was occurring)?

What were your feelings and emotions toward the situation a week later? A month later?

What was the resulting behavior (how did you react)?

How did your reaction impact the results (positively or negatively)?

What was the outcome?

What if you could move through life knowing that absolutely everything happens for a reason and that we have attracted these events into our lives? What if we knew that within every event there was a hidden opportunity that could propel us forward toward our truth and destiny; helping us find happiness, peace and joy? I believe that this is absolutely how life works and that it is our perspective and perception of the world that reflects back to us. If we see the world as a negative place that should be feared, a place where we need to always be looking for the possible problems in every situation, then this is what we will see. Conversely, if we see the beauty, joy and wonder within the world and its events, this is what we will experience. What and how you think about things matters!

# CHAPTER THREE

# THE **BEGINNING** OF SPIRITUALLY ALIGNED LEADERSHIP

**W**hat if you could create a life free of fear, which includes professional challenge, joy and abundance; a life where your influence on those you lead, those in your family and those in your community, is always positive and genuine, and where your relationships are rich and rewarding? What if you could help your employees create a rewarding professional work life which brings them great joy? This is all possible and easier to create than you might think.

First we must do our personal work and begin to lead ourselves before we can consider having an impact on others. It requires a conscious and deliberate approach to everything we do.

## Are You on Auto-Pilot?

Most of us go through life on auto-pilot. We have thoughts and make decisions that are automatic responses to life situations. Often our decisions are heavily affected by what we believe is the *right* decision based on social norms, what we were taught in school or by the expectations of others. Some of these decisions arise out of an immediate reaction, and some we process over a day or two or even longer. Regardless of how they come about, most of these decisions are heavily influenced by outside factors. We are living on auto-pilot.

A simple example might be when someone says something to you that is unkind or you deem as offensive. You might react by being hurt or offended. What is important here is to recognize that you *chose* to be hurt or offended. We would prefer to believe that we are justified in our response and we have no control, but this is simply not true. We have complete control over how we react to life situations. Many of us are pre-programmed through our upbringing to believe that certain things are right and certain things are wrong and that there is an appropriate reaction to every life situation.

When we perceive that we have been wronged, most of us will have a typical response of being hurt, angry or offended. We allow our emotions and the thoughts in our head to come into play so that our reactions to situations are what we would consider typical. For example, we are angry if someone says something that is perceived as hurtful; fearful if someone makes a threat or if there is perceived danger, and sad when someone we love leaves. I am not suggesting that these reactions are wrong or inappropriate, but if they are automatic and fairly instantaneous they may not be conscious, deliberate or well thought-out. They may not serve you well and this is worth consideration.

We absolutely have a choice as to how we react to life situations, but before we can do this successfully, we need to consider other factors—the conversations that we have with ourselves in our head, our emotions, and how we feel in general about our present situation.

## Who's Leading Whom?

I would like you to take a moment and consider how much time you spend leading others. Consider how much time you spend trying to influence, direct or plan the activities of others. How much time do you spend trying to influence your spouse in the direction that you feel is appropriate? How much time do you spend directing and facilitating the lives of your children? How influential are you trying to be with your aging parents?

Most of us spend significant amounts of time directing, leading, planning, and influencing the lives of others. We are involved in our aging parents' lives when trying to facilitate and influence their next life decisions. Then we are also leading and guiding our children in a direction that we feel is appropriate and aligns with what we think is right. Finally we go off to work where we lead, direct, plan, and influence the work and decision-making of our employees. I know that many of you are saying, "But this is the role I play, this is what I'm supposed to do." One of the primary goals of Spiritually Aligned Leadership is to challenge this mindset and to assist leaders in examining their traditional thinking around the role they play in leading others.

If you add up all of the time and energy spent leading other people in your life compared to the amount of time spent leading yourself, you will be shocked to discover that you are the lowest priority. Most of us spend a fraction of our time leading ourselves compared to the amount of time we spend trying to direct other people in our community, families and our businesses. The real question is why? Why do we spend so much time focused on others instead of focused on ourselves?

Another important and yet very difficult question is why do we believe that we have the right to try and significantly lead and influence other people. It seems we believe we have the right answers for other people. Specifically, when we consider our children and our employees, we fundamentally believe we know more or better than they do. My goal is to challenge this thinking and to re-align your focus to becoming the best leader of yourself *and only you*. By doing so, you create the best possible life for yourself while increasing, in a very natural way, your organic influence on others.

When you focus on leading yourself, the rest of the puzzle comes together in a natural and organic way with little or no effort whatsoever. We lose authenticity and integrity when we focus on the outside puzzle pieces while neglecting the most important part of leadership—the leading of one's self. Our employees can see right through this and so can many of the other people in our lives. We often become a walking contradiction, believing we have the right to lead others when in fact we're not intentionally and deliberately leading ourselves.

Sometimes we focus on leading others so intensely because we fundamentally believe they don't have the skills or capacity to lead themselves. This plays out daily with regard to our children. Yet this couldn't be further from the truth. Our children, employees and even most of our elderly parents are more than capable of leading themselves. When we turn inward, and focus on leading ourselves we can begin to see the significant strength and capacity within others.

As a public speaker on the topic of leadership, I often ask the

audience "Who manages you best?" The answer is always the same regardless of the size of the group, "Me of course." So why do we believe this is any different for our employees? They want an opportunity to manage themselves and they are extremely capable of leading themselves. However, just like most of us, they have forgotten how. They are focused on doing what others expect of them, worried about how others will judge them and attempting to make others happy. No wonder many of us are confused. In the corporate environment we have spent the last 100 years teaching people to not think, to not take ownership, to not rely on their own gifts, strengths and know-how. Organizations have especially discouraged employees from going within and tapping into their intuitive side (heart-centered/spiritually grounded) to seek the right answer or right action.

Instead, a climate of fear prevails within companies as employers worry about losing control and employees worry about getting fired if their manager believes they aren't following procedures properly. Again this is based on a belief that people won't do the right thing. In fact some organizations don't even want the employee to do the right thing. This is because the organization, so buried in politics, bureaucracy and legalities, has lost all sense of *what the right thing to do is*. The result is groups of employees continually trying to figure out what the company, manager, or department expect them to do, what process to follow and how to react in every situation. These employees dial down their natural abilities to lead themselves and make great decisions, because it is more important to follow the company line. The overall result is less creativity, less authenticity, less innovation, less authentic engagement, less intellect being shared and the true talent, skills and abilities of each employee are lost. This is one of the key factors leading to reduced productivity and performance. To make a shift in leadership approach, and hence corporate environment, the leader must first recognize that each employee has all of the right answers, is by nature a great person, and that when given the opportunity to self-lead they will have a much better opportunity to make right decisions and take right actions. It must be okay for each employee to dial up their right-brain, heart-centered intuitive self to seek their truth and alignment. It stands to reason that leaders must first learn how to do this for themselves before they can encourage others to do the same. The Spiritually Aligned Leader always sets the example.

This is the fundamental paradigm shift that we ask you to consider—that your employees, children, spouse, and other family members have all of the skills, ability and capacity to lead themselves. In fact it's likely they are seeking the freedom to do just that. I am not suggesting that as a manager, partner or parent you stop being engaged with your employees, spouse or your children, but simply suggest it is about how you engage. We will spend more time on this in subsequent chapters. For now we need to look at some of the factors that require consideration for leading-self.

## Noise: The Conversations with Our Roommate

Our definition of "Noise" is those conversations you have in your head, with yourself or your "Roommate." A reflection on whether these conversations are with yourself, your Ego, or Roommate may become clearer to you as this work unfolds however, at this point it is not overly important what you call the voice in your head. A clear observation of the noise or Roommate in our head is critically important to understanding how we operate, make decisions and often rely on auto-pilot.

For the purposes of this next exercise, let's make a couple of general assumptions. We know that there are twenty-four hours in a day and we are going to assume that the average person gets eight hours of sleep per night. This leaves each person with sixteen hours a day. Now consider, of those sixteen hours, how much time do you have noise (conversations going on) in your head?

If you are like most people, the general response is fifteen hours and fifty minutes or more likely sixteen hours. Some participants in our workshops say, "I constantly have conversations going on with myself." Many people have never even thought about this and it's a bit of a surprise to consider how much activity is actually going on inside their thoughts. I am often asked, "What is wrong with that?" There is nothing fundamentally wrong with having lots of internal conversations, however there are several questions that should be asked and their answers considered. One of the questions I like to ask is "Should the brain be on 24/7 or sixteen hours out of sixteen hours? How do I feel when I have that much noise going on? Do I ever feel simply exhausted?" This is a great time to get out your journal. My challenge to you is throughout each day, stop momentarily over the coming week and consider the following questions. This is not an easy practice and requires discipline and focus. However it will become one of the most important tools to being a Spiritually Aligned Leader.

1. Of the sixteen hours in a day how much of the conversation in my head is positive and how much is negative? I recognize that some of the conversation will be fairly neutral; for example, simple, regular decision-making at work. Negative _____% Positive _____%.

2   How much of my internal conversation brings value into my life?

3. How much of this conversation moves me forward and how much holds me back?

4. And finally and most importantly, how much of the conversation makes me feel good and how much does not? Good_____% Not good _____%.

Our thoughts are an important indicator of how we feel. Why are our thoughts so important and why do they have so much impact on us? These questions can be answered in the next section—the topic of thoughts as energy.

**Thoughts are Energy**

Science has proven that absolutely everything is energy. Energy cannot die; it's all around us. It's part of us. Energy can be slow or fast moving and can vibrate at a high or low frequency.

Even a piece of furniture is energy where the atoms just move very slowly; slower than we can see. Because we can't see the atoms moving, we believe the desk is static, unchanging; when in fact this is not true. Everything comes into form and goes out of form and everything begins as a thought. Someone has a thought to make a desk, build a building or create a new home. Everything begins as a thought and then moves from thought to form either quickly or slowly depending on a number of other factors. This is not hard to believe or imagine as we have all experienced it. We have all had a thought that over time became a reality (taking form) where prior to this it did not exist.

You may wonder what energy has to do with leadership, happiness or effectiveness at work. It has everything to do with it, because every thought you have affects your outcomes. Every thought you have impacts your reactions to life and you have a choice. You can have thoughts that are of a high frequency— extremely positive and open, or negative—low frequency thoughts that eventually will create low frequency, negative results. It's that simple.

Every one of us has experienced this in our daily lives but because we are mostly on auto-pilot, reacting to life situations we assume that our thoughts have nothing to do with a specific outcome. This simply isn't true. Our thoughts have everything to do with outcomes.

Here is another way to look at it. A situation occurs in our environment and we take in that experience. We will have thoughts and opinions about that experience and those thoughts and opinions will create feelings. The feelings we have will then evoke emotions, which can include positive emotions such as joy, thankfulness, peace, patience or they could evoke negative emotions such as fear, anger, frustration, etc. Those emotions affect our behavior and our behavior affects our actions. Our actions affect our outcomes.

Most people look at the figure 1.1 and state, "I agree with this, it makes sense." So even if you don't believe in the concept of "our thoughts are energy" most of us can logically agree that

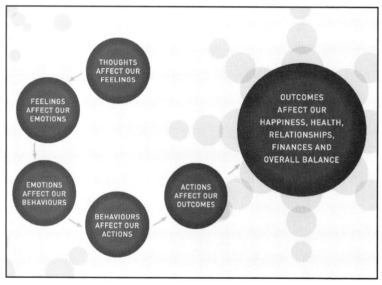

Figure 1.1

what we think about does affect how we feel, which affects our emotional state, which affects our behavior, which affects actions and outcomes. It just makes both intuitive and logical sense (right-brain and left brain are usually okay with this). It is important to note that feelings are different from emotions. When I use the term *feeling* I am referring to the internal sense or feeling a person has about a specific thought. Feelings are closely connected to our thoughts. Emotions, however, are a result of feelings that have been held onto for a long time. Emotions often result in a physiological reaction. This is why monitoring how you feel, and the resulting emotions, is so important.

Those with a strong propensity for left-brain thinking will often decide that, although this depiction is true, if they can control their emotions and not *show* their true feelings they can remove the biases and make better decisions. The problem with this thinking is that hiding and ignoring feelings and emotions does not work. In fact, when they think they are hiding what they truly feel, they are only fooling themselves; everyone around them knows how they really feel without them saying a thing. This is because "thoughts are energy" and everyone can feel the true energy being emitted into the environment, group, team and/or family. This strategy of controlling emotions may work in the short-term, but never works in the long-term.

When leaders consider the logical strategy of burying feelings and emotions to effectively do their jobs they are being dishonest with themselves (remember honesty before kindness) and the end result is additional feelings of frustration, resentment and sometimes anger. You are not hiding anything from family, friends, employers or employees. You are simply masking what will inevitably come to the surface and be revealed. Your energy goes with you everywhere, into every situation and with every encounter, so why not choose the energy you take with you. Why not shift your energy to an energy that serves you and others— be deliberate and intentional in everything you do. Deliberate, conscious and purposeful thoughts, feelings, behaviors and actions produce intentional results.

We also need to consider that the younger generation (our children and employees) are much more intuitive, heart-centered, and many were born with heightened right-brain activity. They are tuned into their feelings and emotions in a much more acute way. While they are capable of invoking left-brain analytical processing, they prefer gut-feel, heart-centered intuition and will lean towards intuitive decision-making. This is one of the main reasons why this younger generation is much less likely to fit into our old mechanistic work environment. If organizations hope to attract the younger talent, they will need to change their entire approach and shift their leadership style.

## It's Not About Positive Thinking

I am often accused of promoting positive thinking as a simple cure-all for changing your life, leadership style etc. This is not true. Positive thinking is important as a starting place, but the real change comes when you can change how you feel; when you replace negative emotions and feelings with positive ones. How you *feel* absolutely matters to the outcomes you get.

Let's take the famous situation of losing weight. Most of us have been in a situation, at one time in our lives, where we commit to going on a diet to lose weight. The first thing we do is decide on all of the things we are going to give up. *I won't do this and I won't do that, I won't eat this and I won't eat that.* How does it feel as you prepare to get rid of many of the foods you love and want each day? We pick a day to begin and we are off. Except that around the entire process is a sense of lack and negative thoughts about what you won't be able to have. Dieting is usually not an inclusive process that allows the person to have countless choices with endless variety, and the focus is usually on what we need to stay away from. Then on day four we eat something that is not on the list or we get on the scale and we have gained half a pound. What is the first thing we say to ourselves? If you are like me you say, "I hate this; no matter what I do, I fail. I can't do this." The next thing we know, we have our face in the ice cream bucket and are pigging out.

Consider Figure 1.1. We have negative thoughts (a sense of lack, what we can't have) we have a minor setback and more negative thoughts; *I can't do this.* The feelings this thinking creates are negative; feelings of not being successful, a failure, evoking negative emotions and then our behaviors are affected, resulting in poor outcomes. This is the cycle that many of us have experienced over and over again.

The thoughts we have are the critical starting place for change, but it is the feelings and resulting emotions that have the most significant impact. It is not about being a positive thinker; it is about going to the next level and feeling what it will be like when you are thin. How great it will feel to have a fabulous day that includes nutritious foods and a successful trip to the gym. You have to move from feeling fat and ugly to feeling beautiful, healthy and fit. Many people will say, "But I am fat, ugly and unfit, so how can I feel any different." It is the story you tell yourself that matters; it is what you say about yourself in your head and more importantly the subsequent feelings you have that are holding you back.

I will share examples of how this works, but for now it is important that you consider your own life, and evaluate yourself in an honest and forthright way. See the exercise below. I am sure most of you have done this type of questionnaire before. You will have seen versions of this in many different books or workshops. However, regardless of how many times or versions you have seen, it is always an important test of evaluating where you are today.

**Personal Evaluation**

Circle which best describes how you feel in each of the following areas of your life. (1 = It couldn't get any worse, things are really bad to 10 = It couldn't get any better, I love this part of my life). Be honest with yourself; you deserve it and are worth the truth.

| | |
|---|---|
| Finances | 1 2 3 4 5 6 7 8 9 10 |
| Health | 1 2 3 4 5 6 7 8 9 10 |
| Relationship | 1 2 3 4 5 6 7 8 9 10 |
| Career | 1 2 3 4 5 6 7 8 9 10 |
| Relationship with Self | 1 2 3 4 5 6 7 8 9 10 |

Some people struggle with scoring the Relationship with Self question. This is because most people have never thought about it. Try to give this a score. Consider how well you know yourself, how much you truly love yourself. Are you absolutely happy with who you are overall? The evaluation for Relationship is usually applied to the respondent's primary relationship in their life (husband, wife, girlfriend, mother).

Once those questions are completed, answer the following:

1. What are the dominant thoughts you have regarding the area in which you scored yourself the lowest?

2. Are these thoughts negative or positive?

3. What feelings and emotions do you have regarding this area of your life?

As someone who has always struggled with her weight, if I had done this test five years ago, I would have scored my health as very low. Not because my health was in jeopardy, but because my body image, thoughts, feeling and emotions were very low regarding this area of my life. I had very negative energy (low frequency) regarding my body image. One day after struggling for years, I simply said, "I have had enough of this negative Nelly stuff. I am going to change how I think about myself, how I feel about my body and my negative emotions toward myself. Instead I will begin to think about how pretty I am and I'll imagine how it will feel when I am healthy, lean and eating better." I never went on a diet and I never gave up anything I loved. Here is what happened.

I met with my son, Geoff, who at the time was a personal trainer, and told him I was done. The negative thinking and feeling was over. I was going to feel better, and have positive emotions around my body image. He said, "Great, now go and get your scale, take it into the parking lot and drive over it, until it is destroyed. Then go throw it in the trash bin." We were living in a condominium at the time, so this was easy to do. Check that box—scale destroyed! I have not been on a scale since that day and have no idea how much I weigh.

Then Geoff said, "No matter what else you do, you must pick one day per week and make it your *fun* day. You must do something really fun which absolutely should include eating anything you want. Go to your favorite restaurant, eat french fries, ice cream and drink beer if that is what you want to do. And finally let's get serious at the gym." The only other advice he gave me was to drink lots of water.

When you read the above, do you see anything in that scenario that comes from a negative, lacking or giving up mentality? The only thing I gave up was the scale and it was a huge relief to know that I never had to get on a scale again. What I weighed just simply didn't matter anymore. It was about how I felt and what I thought about. It was finally all about me. I decided every morning to ensure my thoughts were on feeling great. I monitored what I thought about when it came to my body image. I chose clothes from the closet that I knew would fit well and make me feel good. I started going to the gym and telling myself, *I can do this, I can get strong* and when I looked in the mirror I made sure I told myself how pretty I looked and how wonderful it was going to feel when I had lost weight. I wrote in my journal every night about how much I enjoyed going to the gym and how the food I was putting in my body was going to great use. I wrote about how much I was going to enjoy being able to shop in any store I wanted. I did not go on a diet of any type and I simply drank more water and had my *fun* days. The fascinating thing was I had naturally started to make different choices (behavior/actions) because I had different feelings and emotions about my health and weight. Before I knew it I was not eating red meat, then I stopped eating chicken and eventually had given up all meat and fish. I never decided to become a vegetarian, it was never a conscious decision, it simply happened. I loved salads and avocados and every fruit I could get my hands on. I switched to olive and coconut oil only and removed all processed foods from my diet.

It is important to also note that there was NO calendar. There was no deadline or tracking of how long it took to lose the weight etc. It was not about being on a diet, it was about feeling great.

That was the only focus both internally and externally. But it all started from the *inside*, monitoring my thoughts, which had a huge impact on my feelings, emotions, behaviors, actions and outcomes. Several years later, I have no idea how much I weigh and don't care, but I have replaced my wardrobe four times and am about to do it again. I love the gym, walking, sailing and being in nature and love the fact that I am extremely close to being a vegan. The only reason I am not a full-on vegan is I simply don't want to deprive myself or give up anything I love, and I love Greek yogurt. As long as I *feel* that way I will continue to eat my Greek yogurt whenever I want. Oh, and I also gave up alcohol, which surprised me because I love a cold beer on a hot day; but it just seemed natural and easy to do.

It is time to get deeper into your own evaluation and your own processes. Consider how you scored yourself in the earlier survey and answer the following questions:

1. How could you change your thoughts in the area in which you scored yourself the lowest? What would you need to do?

2. What are the specific new thoughts you could have every day regarding this area of your life?

If you want to change the results or level of happiness in this area you MUST change your thoughts first; then connect to a better feeling (about this area) through those thoughts. Remember, how you *feel* is the most important thing.

1. What would you need to do to change how you feel about this area of your life? Consider things like your imagination and storytelling.

2. What are your improved desires relating to this area? What do you see in the future?

3. What will it feel like and how will your life be when you have fully realized this desire and intention?

Further consideration must be given to the fact that the area in which you scored yourself the lowest is impacting all other areas of your life. Intuitively, you already know this to be true. As you increase your positive energy in that area, the others will begin to improve organically. It's like magic! Once you have applied the fundamental principles in the area of your life where you are struggling, all other areas can easily be increased in vibrational frequency (positive energy) by applying the same strategy.

If finances are your struggle, you need to fully evaluate what you think about and how you feel about money. You will always lack money and have financial challenges if you continually tell yourself that you don't have enough money. You need to imagine a life full of abundance. You need to have an abundance or appreciation journal where you track all of the amazing things you have in your life. You need to shift your thinking, which will change how you feel. Before you know it, you will be passing by the items in the store window saying to yourself, *I could buy that if I wanted to, but I choose not to, as I don't need anything and know that more stuff will not make me happy.*

**A Business Journey**

Applying these principles in both our personal and professional lives is important so that we can clearly see how all of the dots connect to *leading-self.* Several years ago, I decided that I wanted a business partner with a specific skill set who could move our organization forward in a new area of Human Resource Management. As a result, I set out to find a person who would buy into the business. I will explain later why this was my first mistake. For now, it is the parts of the story that connect to how we react to unwanted events that matter.

I found this smart, talented and successful gentleman, Andy. He had a long history of working in a large organization and had exactly the skill-set we were looking for. He had great business connections and wanted to be an owner. I thought I had done my homework and due diligence when screening this potential business partner, but I quickly learned that I had not. We began to negotiate, have the business appraised, and agree on shares to be purchased and future share options. He joined our organization in May and by the end of September of that same year, I could tell that things were in trouble. It is important to note that we had just spent a significant amount of money on a very complex and detailed shareholders agreement, and I was hopeful that this was the person who could assist in taking us into new business areas. I had made tons of mistakes.

Early on in the partnership we had some significant and unforeseen events happen that strained the business in a way we had never experienced before or could have anticipated. I was used to the dynamism of entrepreneurship, but the new business partner was not and things got very rocky. Fear set in and looking back I can only imagine the type of conversations taking place in my partner's head. When I later reviewed emails and letters it was clear he was so unhappy and believed that I had completely misled him.

Instead of speaking with me and working through the fear and anxiety, he chose to go within his mind and create all kinds of stories about me and the business. Before I knew it we were no longer business partners, but estranged. After more than a month of trying to open up conversation with him, on December 23rd of that same year, I received a thirteen page facsimile from Andy's lawyer (someone I had never heard of previously) accusing me of all kinds of inappropriate and unethical behavior. I was being threatened with a lawsuit. I immediately contacted our corporate lawyer and the fun began.

So why do I tell this story? I tell this story because on the eve of Christmas and a two-week break from work, I received a threat of lawsuit and had just lost my business partner. Less than six months earlier I had spent significant amounts of money to put in place a comprehensive shareholders' agreement, which was now being completely ignored. I remember hiding out in my home office on Christmas day, talking to my lawyer, while I was supposed to be at the dinner table. I was trying to pretend that nothing was wrong and that everything was okay. We could easily have lost everything.

My husband and I sat down on Boxing Day and had a lengthy discussion about how to proceed. We made a decision that under no circumstances would we become negative, have negative feelings toward Andy and that we would look for every opportunity to feel okay with what was happening. At this point in our lives we had already done some significant shifting in our energy and knew that to navigate through these types of situations you had to look for every opportunity to learn. I asked myself every day, *Where is our learning opportunity? How can I gain personal growth through this situation?*

As the weeks progressed, the more positive and balanced we became, the more Andy's negative energy increased. The legal conversations seemed never-ending. Costs were mounting and little progress was being made. I continued to monitor the conversation in my head and tried every day to send good energy to Andy in hopes that he would find some relief. I had huge empathy for Andy's situation knowing that he had invested a lot of money into the deal and had huge buyer's remorse. Of course, through any situation like this, you learn a lot of information about the other person, and as a result it became more apparent every day why this happened and why Andy would react the way he did.

We stayed true to our original decision, believing and imagining a positive outcome to the situation. I was able to focus on the business needs throughout the challenge, because I would not allow myself to have negative and unproductive conversations with my Roommate or Ego. I focused on what was important to running the business and, in fact, during that period of time we were awarded a very large contract that resolved several of the issues that we had been plagued with in the previous six months. Our positive energy, as a result of our optimistic thinking and feeling, resulted in a very positive outcome.

There was no lawsuit filed and we met our obligation exactly as was laid out in the shareholders' agreement—which is why you have a shareholders' agreement in the first place. I never regretted the money required for legal support, as they were fabulous to us, and we experienced significant learning. However, I suspected that Andy was having substantial negative conversations with himself, which potentially led him to spending money on lawyers when we already had appropriate escape clauses and processes for us as partners to disengage. It was apparent that he had created a story in his head about how horrible we were and how we would never let him out of the agreement. He felt that because we were so horrible, he should be entitled to more than what was agreed to in the contracts. Instead of following the processes that were already laid out in the agreement, money was spent on both sides to come to the exact same outcome that could have been obtained without the additional legal involvement. It was a great learning opportunity.

We had to monitor our feelings every step of the way. We had to catch ourselves when we started to get negative and we had to shift our thinking toward positive outcomes. I wrote in my journal every night about how I looked forward to a positive and mutually beneficial outcome. Not easy to do under the circumstances and certainly we were not perfect, but we worked every day at controlling the conversations we had in our head.

What you think about absolutely impacts how you feel and how you feel absolutely matters. This is the single most important step in shifting to positive energy and is the beginning of Spiritually Aligned Leadership.

**A Personal Journey**

As you can tell, Spiritually Aligned Leadership and the ability to create positive energy has everything to do with leading-self in all areas of your life. It affects your organizational, family and community leadership approach and as such I like to provide relevant examples from all perspectives.

As a parent, I have learned to rely on Spiritually Aligned

practices as a key strategy for being the mother that I truly want to be. As I share this next example I want you to consider Figure 1.1 again and how our thoughts can dramatically affect our feelings, emotions and behaviors.

Several years ago my beautiful, middle son, Scott had some personal issues, which my husband and I did a poor job of recognizing in a timely manner. He'd had a tough year, losing a personal friend in a car accident, breaking up with an abusive girlfriend and finding himself in a position where he had to move back home. He is a beautiful, creative and sensitive person who is introverted and quiet by nature; a talented writer and performer who never wanted to lead what might be considered a traditional life, but who wanted to act, perform and write. Sandwiched between two other brothers who were very different, extroverted, outgoing and more traditional at the time (not so much now), I believe Scott felt that he was less successful or maybe his parents were not proud of him. As parents we often don't consider the world through the eyes of our children until we are forced to.

We could tell that Scott was not very happy, but we never imagined what was to come. Shortly after Scott moved home, he began to date a new girl. We were always excited when one of our boys brought a girlfriend home, as we had never had any daughters, and we loved the idea of having women in our family. My husband and I tried to be very open and welcoming to each new friend we were introduced to. We always shared the traditional Sunday night dinner and on most Sundays and special occasions, the girlfriends would join us. This girlfriend was different. Very quickly we realized that she didn't want anything to do with us. She attended one dinner and then we never saw her again. However, Scott continued to date her. Slowly Scott stopped attending dinners with us. He had less and less time for his brothers, which was very unusual as he and his brothers had always been very close; each of them only two years apart. They had always been each other's good friends, celebrated birthdays, shared stories and supported each other through good and bad times, but now Scott had no interest in sharing his life with either his parents or his brothers.

One day Scott asked us if we would support his decision to meet with a therapist so that he could work through some issues. My husband and I are huge believers in seeking support and help, from wherever you need it. Scott set up the appointments at a clinic of his choice and we began to pay for it. Our Visa was charged twice monthly for many months, so we knew he was attending meetings on a regular basis.

We began to get weird and disturbing emails from his girlfriend advising that we didn't really know Scott and that the only person who could help Scott was her. She told us that Scott did not want anything to do with us or his brothers and that she would be the only person in his life. By this time things had deteriorated further. Scott had gone to the family doctor and was immediately put on anti-depressants. Scott was numb and we were losing the son we had known for twenty-three years. His smile was gone, his creative and amazing wit had disappeared and he was quickly becoming unrecognizable to us.

Scott continued to live in his bedroom in the basement, but there was no interaction with the family. There was no communication and he did not attend any family events. We barely saw him as he moved from his car in the driveway to his bedroom and back to his car. His phone would ring. It would be a call from his girlfriend, and he would jump and be gone in a second. He never had any money and yet he worked two jobs and was tired all of the time. He was completely disengaged from the whole family.

His brothers were devastated, not understanding what was happening and why. His older brother, Geoff, cried almost every day for months and Mike just went inside choosing to try and ignore the overwhelming dysfunction playing out within our family. We decided to seek family therapy as a way of working through all of our emotions and thoughts around the situation. The four of us went off to counseling every week for over a month to try and come to terms with what was going on. We had been living this nightmare for over eight months and things were getting worse instead of better.

I want you to take a moment and think about what the counseling sessions were like. What do you think we talked about? What was the focus and how did it unfold? Then I want you to review Figure 1.1 and consider what the thoughts were going through my head? What were the conversations I was having with my Roommate? What were the conversations my other two sons and husband were having with themselves? What were the resulting emotions and feelings and ultimate behaviors that transpired? How would you feel? What stories would you potentially tell yourself? Imagine some of the thoughts I had about the new girlfriend, her influence, her family? What things might I have wanted to do?

Every counseling session was dark, negative and full of storytelling. Each family member shared how horrible they felt and helpless they were to make things better. There was anger, frustration, huge amounts of grief and I know that our oldest son was truly grieving the loss of his brother, thinking that Scott would never come back.

At one point I was sure that Scott was suicidal. My husband and I were desperate to help; we had tried everything and nothing was working. Emotions were out of control and the life we had known for twenty-three years was over, never to be the same. I remember coming home from work one day and the tears would not stop. I could no longer drive and I had to stop at the side of the road. I was sure we were going to lose our beautiful Scott. I decided to call the clinic where Scott continued to get counseling. They were absolutely of no help, not wishing to speak with us and stating over and over again "we can't discuss Scott with you; we can't tell you anything." I begged one of the doctors, (not Scott's therapist, as Scott was an adult, we weren't allowed to speak with her due to privacy laws) to give me any information and to at least take into consideration what I knew. I begged her to consider that Scott was suicidal and that we needed a more aggressive intervention NOW. After twenty minutes of desperate pleading, the therapist on the other end of the phone simply said, "You may have to get used to the idea that you have lost him already."

I was done! I hung up the phone and knew that I was spent... there was nothing left, just a deep dark hole. I don't know how long I sat in my car, but it seemed forever before I could compose myself enough to drive home.

What we think about affects how we feel and how we feel affects our emotions, which affects our behaviors and actions and ultimately affects outcomes. The outcome was not looking good!

Everything I know to be true has been learned through experience first-hand, professional, personal and otherwise. Back then I didn't know that every unwanted, undesired event is an opportunity presented in magical form to shift who we are to a better and more complete state. Although I had begun my spiritual journey, I had not been deliberately practicing the Tools of Intention. I now know we have to believe that we have all the answers we need on the inside; we have to be willing to look inside and be brutally honest with ourselves; willing to seek the opportunity in every experience even when it feels excruciating.

# PART II

# THE TREE OF ABUNDANCE
# AND TOOLS OF INTENTION

# CHAPTER FOUR

# THE TREE OF ABUNDANCE AND TOOLS OF INTENTION

The practice of creating positive energy and becoming a Spiritually Aligned Leader is a journey and not a destination. There is no finish line and, as a result, this way of life is about continuous evolution, growth and depth. It is a practice with significant and profound rewards including an ever-increasing sense of balance, peace, joy, and abundance. Over time the practice becomes second nature and life flows with ease, full of manifested desires, alignment and organic influence. So how do we begin our practice?

Over the next few chapters we will look at the Tools of Intention, but first we need to take a look at the Tree of Abundance; a dynamic representation of the journey to becoming a Spiritually Aligned Leader.

Looking at the Tree of Abundance, we can see three distinct areas of our life that assist us in manifesting all of the desires and intentions we have for ourselves. When all components of the tree are understood and practiced, we are able to gracefully move through life's challenges, seeking only the opportunities for learning and evolution and avoiding the dramas that keep us trapped in past conditioning.

## Understanding the Tree

### The Trunk

I like to start in the middle. The trunk of the tree represents the journey that each of us is on. The journey is unique to each person, but requires similar skills if we are to navigate life's challenges and opportunities from a healthy, resilient and Spiritually Aligned perspective.

Cut open the trunk of a tree and you will see growth rings; each ring representing a year in the life of the tree. Each year might include warm sunshine, rain, wind, snow, heavy sleet; some rings may also include the memories of tornadoes, and hurricanes. The rings in the tree are symbolic of the years of our lives, full of events that include beautiful moments of joy and abundance, as well as difficulties and tragedies. The trunk represents the milestones that you experience; the desired and undesired events. Your wedding day might be one of those days, the birth of a child or the loss of a dear friend. It could also be the day the divorce was final or your child's graduation; those moments in life where the world can take your breath away or stop you cold. It can even be, as in in my case, the day you get fired. We all have a story that is full of desired and undesired events along with negative and positive events. The Tree Trunk represents all of it. It is "The Journey."

## The Top of the Tree

The top of the tree represents the rewards that come when a person practices Spiritually Aligned Leadership and is represented by the health of the leaves and branches. When a tree is unhealthy the leaves lack brightness and vibrancy, they droop and point toward the ground. When a tree is healthy, strong and balanced with enough sun, rain and nutrients (gathered from the roots), you can see it clearly. The leaves are bright, full of color and pointing to the sky, seeking the rays of the sun. This is the same energy that Spiritually Aligned Leaders emit every day. They are balanced, strong and seeking the brightness in everything. They seek the goodness, strengths and positive attributes in every person and every situation.

Spiritually Aligned Leaders are grateful for the abundance they have in their lives and they know that through their positive thoughts, feelings and emotions they co-create everything that comes into their life. They take responsibility for results and avoid victim mentality. They are change agents in the world creating positive energy with everyone and everything they touch. This may seem like a tall order, but in fact when the Tools of Intention are practiced, it becomes easier and easier to be the change you want to see. You build organic influence with little effort and your leadership is noticed in all areas of your life. Relationships improve with your spouse, children, organization, clients, and your immediate supervisor. People seek your advice and counsel and you become the coach and coachee (continuous learner) in all areas of your life. Along the way you will discover your higher purpose and you will become incredibly confident in who you are, where you are going and what you are capable of accomplishing. You will do all of this while reducing the Ego and its negative impacts.

It is however, *a practice*. It is not a destination. You will not hit a finish line. As soon as you get close to the finish line it will move. We are not intended, as a species, to *arrive*. Some of you might still be thinking things like, *If only I had more money, I would be happy; life will be complete*. You might be thinking, *When I get that perfect job, I will be happy and fulfilled*. All of this thinking is *old* thinking. We are not supposed to cross the proverbial finish line; we are designed for continuous growth and evolution. Most of us intuitively know this; however, we don't think about it much because of the influences of our present society.

Many of us still believe that there is a good, right or wrong way of being and that when we attain or accomplish certain goals, we will have made it. We continue to look for external things to complete us when the answers lie within. Money, possessions, relationships, marriage and children cannot complete us. Our completeness lies within our ability to tap into our own internal source energy; to tap into our heart-center and to seek our unique joy. As we tap into our heart-center and learn to seek the answers from within, we become Spiritually Aligned Leaders. When we become Spiritually Aligned Leaders, the things we seek, manifest with ease. We build healthy and joyful relationships, and are grateful for the abundance appearing in our life. We find joy in very simple things and balance and peace are independent of any possession, relationship or sense of material abundance. They are simply results of living and being a Spiritually Aligned Leader.

As a corporate leader, this information is incredibly profound because as you become spiritually aligned you live and practice the Tools of Intention every day. This becomes a way of being. As you become consistent in your approach, your employees know what to expect. You will seek to find the greatness in each employee *all* of the time. You will encourage them, with little effort, to seek their own joy and passions, and as you do this, they then begin to ask themselves the hard questions about their own life. You become the catalyst for significant change within your organization, company, department or team depending on where you are in the organizational chart.

Go within and the answers will appear. The Tools of Intention assist a person with *going within*, to become self-reliant and to lead-self in all of life's situations. Spiritually Aligned Leaders self-empower. They never look to others to provide their internal fuel. Their power comes from deep inside and this positive energy cannot be destroyed. Let's look at each of the Tools of Intention and begin to build our Tree of Abundance.

### *The Roots of the Tree*

The roots are there to take in nourishment, water, and nutrients from the soil. The roots of the tree support the trunk and branches, and they must be healthy, strong and able to do their job if the tree is to withstand life's events. The ability for the roots to capture, gather and store nutrients is one of the determining factors of the health of the tree. When the roots are firmly grounded and strong, the tree can withstand the more difficult storms. We use this analogy of the roots of the tree to represent the Tools of Intention. Each root represents a tool or practice that will assist you in building a strong foundation that is grounded, consistent and stable and will allow you to flourish in all areas of your life.

The Tools of Intention are practices of Spiritually Aligned Leaders, used throughout their personal and professional lives. It does not matter whether you are playing the role of CEO, department manager, mother, father, brother, sister or Board of

Director, the Tools of Intention are incorporated throughout everything you think, feel and act upon. The practice is consistent across situations, events and obstacles regardless of how difficult and the rewards are almost inconceivable; a life that is blissful, balanced and full of abundant joy.

You can begin to see the connections between the roots of the tree and the trunk. With the Tools of Intention (roots) we are able to bend and move through the desired events in our lives and also the challenges (the rings in the trunk of the tree) with minimal effort and stress. More importantly, because we are co-creators of our world (what we think about and do mirrors back at us) and because our thoughts are energy, as we begin to practice the Tools of Intention the undesired and unwanted events become fewer and fewer. *The better it gets the better it gets.* Applying the Tools of Intention in every situation, allows the individual leader, parent, teacher, friend to navigate life with ease and grace.

This approach to life builds a natural and organic influence about which others become very curious. They want to know how to create this in their own lives. They want to be around the Spiritually Aligned Leader and to be influenced by their balanced and positive approach to life.

The Tools of Intention include the following practices:

▶ Becoming The Observer

▶ Non-judgment

▶ Meditation

▶ Understanding and Dealing with Karma

▶ Conscious Presence

- ▶ Gratitude and Appreciation

- ▶ Acceptance

- ▶ Detachment

- ▶ Forgiveness

- ▶ Alignment

- ▶ Purpose

In subsequent chapters, each of these topics will be explored in detail. You will learn the fundamentals of practicing each tool and how to recognize when you are out of alignment. You will get an opportunity to build a plan that focuses on the most important relationship you will ever have—*the one with yourself!*

# CHAPTER FIVE

# THE OBSERVER

Becoming the Observer is one of the first tools that a person should practice as they embark on the journey of Spiritually Aligned Leadership. Whether you look at this material from your perspective as a business leader, parent or any other role you might play, the Observer should show up in everything you do. In this chapter we will discuss the Observer from two distinct vantage points. The first centers on becoming the Observer of YOU. This practice fosters your ability to lead from within and awakens your receptivity to your inner guidance. The second practice involves becoming the Observer of the World. Both will reap rewards in your life.

## Becoming the Observer of YOU

Becoming the Observer of YOU means that you begin to observe your thoughts, feelings, emotions and behaviors, in all areas of your life. It means taking a 35,000 foot view of yourself and monitoring what shows up in your life by asking the following questions: What thoughts am I having right now? How do I feel? What emotions and behaviors are arising as a result of what I am thinking and feeling?

This may seem to be an odd concept, but as you monitor the ongoing conversation you have with your Roommate, Ego or yourself, (depending on how you view your internal dialogue), you can assess its value and contribution to your emotional well-being. Do your thoughts serve you? Do they make you feel good and move you forward in the direction you want to go? If the answer is *no* you can make a different choice and change what you are thinking about. However, if you do not become the Observer, then you cannot monitor these conversations and are not making a choice. You are subject to auto-pilot.

At the center of all successful and joyful leaders, parents and teachers is a Spiritually Aligned individual who observes and monitors, in an intentional and deliberate way, what they are thinking about. They observe the subsequent energy they are putting out and the feelings that they create within themselves. They lead from within at every stage of their day.

Sometimes it takes a crisis or a bump in the road for an individual to embrace this practice and observe themselves in this intentional way. In my case this happened when I was fired from my job; the universe demanded that I take the time to evaluate what I had been thinking and feeling throughout that time period. The universe mirrors back to us and provides situations and experiences that align with what we have been thinking about and more importantly *feeling*. Prior to losing my job, I had been very unhappy with something that had been occurring within the organization. I was frustrated and not feeling in alignment. At the time, however, I was not honest with myself about this and I wanted to believe that everything would work out, but inside I did not feel this way. As I look back, it is apparent that I was not meant to be there for a long time and that my philosophy and beliefs about organizational life were in direct opposition to that of this organization.

Any time an undesired event arrives in our lives, we need to evaluate what we were thinking and feeling at the time. Remember, our natural inclination is to blame other people, the situation, or the world in general. If we are truly honest with ourselves and aware of this information, we do a full evaluation. We will discover that our thoughts and feelings leading up to the event were directly in line with the results we received. When a person continually thinks about how fat and unattractive they are, it can only result in feeling negative about their body, and they will continue to have behavior that aligns with this feeling; behavior like overeating or eating the wrong things.

As you practice the skills of becoming the Observer of YOU, you will soon find yourself observing in a proactive and intentional way. You can then catch yourself when you don't feel right, when you feel off balance or when your emotions seem less than positive. Stop and ask yourself: Why am I feeling off? Why does this not feel right? Why am I emotional about this? This is a fabulous process for growth and self-awareness—as you monitor how you feel, you can intercept the feeling before it manifests as a behavior. Maybe you are having a negative thought about another person or a situation at work. You might be having a negative, inner dialogue with your Roommate about one of your children. Catch yourself then and ask, how does this conversation I am having with my Ego, about this person or this situation, serve me. Note, that I have not mentioned observing others. That is not your job. Your job is to lead yourself and allow others to do the same. Focus on your thoughts, feelings and emotions and no one else's. Recognize that the relationship you have with yourself is the most important relationship and that this is where your focus *must* be if you are to become the best you can be, connected to your true nature.

Before you know it, you will be monitoring your thoughts on a regular basis and catching yourself long before negative feelings, emotions or derailed behavior can manifest. You will have become the Observer. This is not hard to learn, but it does take commitment and resolve in knowing that you absolutely have complete control over what you think about and your resulting feelings.

I have coached and worked with many leaders who honestly believe that what they think about does not affect those in their work environment. I would agree that what they think about has more impact on themselves than on others. However, if a leader thinks that they are 100% successful in hiding how they truly feel about a situation, just because they do not talk about it, they are sadly mistaken. Those around them will feel their energy, either positive or negative, and it will impact whatever situation is unfolding. This also goes for parents who believe they are hiding their true feelings from their children. We cannot completely hide what we are feeling. Most of us will agree that very young children are highly sensitive to the energy of their parents' feelings. I believe this also applies to the younger generation entering the workforce and interacting with their leaders. This increased awareness and sensitivity in young people is due to the fact that they have been exposed to the dogma of life for a shorter period of time. We will touch on this again in subsequent chapters. Regardless, do not believe for a moment that you can hide what you are thinking about just because you have not spoken those thoughts or feelings out loud.

**Trusting your Inner Guidance**

Most people don't suddenly become great at monitoring their thoughts and tuning in to how they feel; especially when we have been relying on other senses and skills to make decisions. Many of us are very left-brain dominant, relying on what the evidence or data tells us about a situation. We live in a society that encourages us to analyze everything to death. I am suggesting that we dial up and monitor how we feel. It is a fabulous indicator of whether we are in alignment or not. It is an internal system (ability) we all have, which for most of us has been discounted and underutilized over the past 100 years. It is time to get back in touch with our inner truth.

Have you ever done something or made a decision that at the time you knew you shouldn't make, but you did it anyway. Your internal sensors were trying to tell you to go in a specific direction, or more importantly to not go in a certain direction, and yet you did anyway. You did not listen to the internal messaging that was being provided to you. We have all received these messages, but again, we have learned to rely on left-brain thinking instead of heart-centered feeling, and so we ignore them. The messaging often comes in negative thinking, a feeling in the pit of your stomach, a headache or anything that feels off to you. Becoming the Observer gives one the ability to tune into this innate guidance system.

I have had several situations where I did not listen to my inner voice, my internal guidance, and because of this I created a negative situation for myself. How I felt about it mirrored back at me. One such example was a vacation I booked a few years ago. I booked it even though I felt like I shouldn't. I allowed the dialogue in my head to overshadow the feelings I had about the trip and it resulted in the booking of a vacation that was very expensive, during a very busy time that took me away from some important activities. The result was some missed opportunities and I also became angry with myself for overspending.

There have been lots of times where I have listened to my inner guidance, such as when I told my husband about not wanting to build a home. Every time I have observed how I felt, asked the important questions about why, was honest with myself and acted on it appropriately, I have been rewarded. As you turn inward and intentionally chose to lead yourself from within, you begin to make right decisions.

A great example of a parent intentionally leading from within can be found in the memoir *The Spark,* written by Kristin Barnett. She writes about her son's journey with autism and how she made the very tough decision to listen to her feelings and go against conventional wisdom as she navigated the challenges of raising him. Imagine how difficult it would be to make the decision to not follow the recommended therapy and follow your own feelings and intuition about how to assist your child. When the medical field, neighbors and family think you should do one thing, but you *feel* you need to do something else, this takes significant courage. Her's is an inspiring story with a fabulous ending.

I know that when raising my own children, I made one mistake after another, reacting to what we were *supposed to do* and not what I felt we should do. Back then I was so out of tune with how I felt, that I made decisions based on what was considered the generally acceptable practice in society. I was on auto-pilot. Our youngest son, Mike, struggled with learning in the traditional way. His extraordinary energy for life and his ability to connect with people was obvious from a very early age. However, due to his high energy he lacked the prescribed ability to sit still and commit to traditional learning methods. Deep in the back of my mind I knew he was exceptional in many ways, however that is not what I thought about or felt most of the time. All I could focus on was his inability to fit in and learn to read and write on the timelines prescribed by the school system.

What message do you think Mike received as we focused on his learning needs, moving him from one school to another, hiring tutors and paying for special after-school classes? Remember what we think about affects how we feel, which affects our emotions and eventually affects our behavior and those around us. From our behavior, and that of the schools', Mike learned that he had a problem—that he was behind, that he was not smart enough. The truth was that Mike was incredibly smart, capable and had gifts that were extraordinary. It is only now in his mid-twenties that he is truly exploring those gifts to their fullest potential. He spent many years struggling, feeling like he was not good enough and believing he needed to prove himself to others. The thoughts, feelings and emotions he had, created specific behaviors. The outcome was that Mike internalized this as a belief that he was not smart enough and that he didn't fit in. He began to have thoughts of inadequacies and those thoughts created feelings and emotions. He created a massive Ego to hide the insecurity. Some of Mike's behavior in his teenage years was very risky and unhealthy. At the age of twenty-six, Mike now speaks openly to people about *his story* and how what we did impacted that story and shaped his life for many years. Our negative thinking and focusing on what Mike could not do, ultimately affected Mike and ignored what he could do.

Being a Spiritually Aligned Parent means that you absolutely monitor what you think about as it relates to your children and you choose the best thoughts and feelings *all of the time*. In a later chapter we will discuss specifically the parent/child relationship and how parents need to create positive energy at all phases of a child's life to allow them to tap into their own inner thoughts, feelings and true nature.

These same philosophies apply to organizational leaders working with employees and team members. Becoming a Spiritually Aligned Leader means that you monitor, all of the time, what you think about and feel relating to your employees and you choose better feeling thoughts. I know this might seem very strange and inappropriate in a business context, because we are taught to work with the facts and only the facts (left-brain) and to evaluate based on evidence and key indicators, but when we do this we miss a huge amount of information that is available to us.

I recently had a director in a large corporation, who after completing one of our courses, realized that this is exactly what she had done with one of her managers. After a couple of negative incidents she was primarily focused on the manager's shortcomings. She struggled to see all of the great gifts he had. She made the decision to observe her thoughts and feelings about this particular manager and what she discovered was that this manager was giving her exactly what she was thinking about, feeling and subconsciously looking for. She decided to change what she thought about and seek evidence about what this manager did well and what his talents were. Before she knew it, she was seeing this manager in a completely different light and was now able to direct him in a different way. Instead of looking for his shortcomings, she was seeking his gifts and talents and was asking him very different questions. She was leading herself intentionally and was now finding ways to work with this manager in a much more positive way. The result was dramatically improved performance by this manager and a new openness to discussing any shortcomings. As she set a great example of leading herself, he began to follow suit and some of the previous issues were now being addressed with no intervention by the director.

## Daily Practices

Many people find that setting aside a journal to record their observations is of great benefit. Use it at the end of each day and write down instances when you were having negative thoughts about yourself or others. Or consider carrying a small notebook with you to jot down every time you are a successful Observer of your thoughts and feelings. We call this *catching ourselves.* Every time you catch yourself (observe yourself) you are one step closer to finding your true nature (true alignment). As you record successful moments you continue to reaffirm your ability to be the Observer of YOU.

The goal is to catch yourself as early as possible, before your negative thinking impacts your behavior. At first you will recognize your thoughts after the fact, but if you embrace this practice it soon becomes quite natural and you will spot your negative thinking early enough to make the choice to adjust your thoughts. When you do this you can avoid negative emotions and possible behavior, which is not in alignment with what you truly want. Remember that *how you feel matters*, so you have to begin to observe how you feel and *catch yourself.*

We have discussed journaling as a way of becoming a better Observer. Meditation is another fabulous tool to truly connect on the inside. There are tons of books on meditation and a wide variety of types of mediation; all of which are great. There is not one right way to meditate, so don't be afraid to experiment. The benefits of meditation are astounding. Meditation has been proven to have positive overall effects on the mind and body and spiritual well-being and has changed many people's lives.

Some of our corporate clients have put meditation rooms into their buildings as a way of providing a quiet, safe place for employees and leaders to clear their minds and prepare for the day, upcoming meetings or simply to become more conscious and present-minded at work. As a person uses meditation to quiet the mind, and connect to their inner self, they become a better Observer of their thoughts and feelings and the result is they also become more present-minded and conscious in all interactions. The individual becomes able to *lead-self* more effectively and more often and there is less and less reacting to life's situations on auto-pilot.

Meditation assists individuals to become conscious and present-minded with every important interaction. You are present while at the grocery store. You remember faces and names and you always slow down when interacting with people who work in the service industry and hospitality. You ensure that they feel your positive energy and know that you appreciate their attention to your needs.

For fun, consider how many conversations you had yesterday. Were you at work going from one meeting to the next? Were you busy shopping and moving from one store to the next? How many of the conversations you had yesterday do you actually remember? Do you remember the person's face or what you talked about? Do you remember smiling at them and ensuring that the energy you brought into the discussion was positive and felt good as well as the energy you left with? When you begin to do this you are becoming conscious and present-minded. Interactions matter. Even those interactions that are seemingly unimportant become very important because the energy you put out comes back to you.

When a person becomes present-minded and fully conscious of themselves they are better able to be a good Observer of what they think about and how they feel. This is because they are not only present on the outside with other people, but they are present within themselves.

If you have ever met a very present-minded leader or worked for someone who is, you quickly see that everything is considered carefully and from within. It is not all about the facts and data (outside world), but is also about how they feel. They slow down and consider carefully every conversation, every interaction and every opportunity to connect. When you work with this person you always leave feeling better, you feel that they made a true effort to connect in a meaningful way. You felt heard. This is because they are present and conscious in every interaction.

A daily practice of journaling, meditation and practicing being present and conscious will assist you in becoming a fabulous Observer of YOU.

## Becoming the Observer of the World

As you become a good Observer of your own thoughts and feelings you will also want to become an Observer of the world. Imagine the world, or your own immediate environment, as an auditorium. This auditorium is very large with a massive stage and hundreds of thousands of seats in the audience. Every person has their very own seat in the audience, which is dedicated to them only. The drama of life is taking place on the stage, right in front of us—all those situations unfolding at work, home, school, all those events occurring in our communities. Each of us sits in our personalized seat and watches the drama. We have a choice. We can step onto the stage and engage in the drama or we can choose to stay in our seat and watch from the audience. The more you observe life unfold and become conscious and present-minded, the more you will intentionally and deliberately choose when to step onto the stage. Your actions will be guided by your inner guidance or that gut-feel, inner voice. As the Observer, you are monitoring your thoughts and feelings and you are deliberating choosing what you think about and how you feel; you then begin to deliberately choose when to engage in the drama of life and when not to. This is when you begin to make significant shifts in your life.

Being engaged in life is fabulous and very important; however, you want to be intentional in your engagement. Consider a situation at work or home that needs your attention. When you carefully and intentionally observe the environment, and then decide when and how to interact and contribute, you are much more likely to be successful. You make a conscious choice to step onto the stage and interact and then you quietly return to your seat in the audience.

A Spiritually Aligned Leader goes within and engages the heart-center when making decisions; they observe what they are thinking about (left-brain/right-brain) and then they consider how they feel. They ask the questions: Is what I am about to do going to make me feel good? Does it feel right and does it come from good intention and from a place of non-Ego? Does it move me forward in a positive way? If the answers are *no,* the Spiritually Aligned Leader will not react. Instead they will go back and dig deeper for the right answers. Remembering *how you feel* or *will feel* after making a decision is very important to being Spiritually Aligned. Decisions are not made from a place of Ego or needing to be right. The Spiritually Aligned Leader will seek their heart-center and choose better feeling thoughts and actions before stepping onto the stage.

We all know people who are on the stage ninety percent of the time, participating in the drama, on auto-pilot as they react to situations in their outer world. They are not monitoring their thoughts, feelings or emotions and, as a result, their behavior is often not in alignment with what they know to be true. They are not intentionally choosing what they think about or how they feel. They are simply reacting to life and often develop a victim mentality. Nothing ever goes right, the glass is always half empty and there is a problem around every corner.

This is often referred to as being *of the world* which is very different than being *in the world*. When we are *of the world* we are interacting and participating which is a good thing, however, if we are *of the world* all the time we cannot observe the world for ourselves. When we are simply *in the world*, we can be the Observer, both internally and externally, and make intentional and deliberate choices when to be *of the world*.

Becoming the Observer of yourself and the world around you is an important tool to becoming and staying a Spiritually Aligned Leader. You monitor the thoughts, feelings and resulting emotions that you have. You *catch yourself* by using how you feel as an indicator as to whether you are in alignment and leading-self. Sometimes this means not doing what others expect and not always following the system, dogma or rules. You observe the world and strategically and intentionally decide when to step onto the stage and be *of the world*, and when to simply sit in your seat and *be in the world*. Everything is a choice, but first you have to become the Observer so that you can make right choices in an intentional and deliberate way. Dial up the heart-center and rely more on what you feel on the inside instead of simply doing what society or others around you think you should do. Lead yourself first. Remember that you are on your own journey and you are not supposed to be on anyone else's journey (don't climb someone else's tree). Stay focused on your journey by leading-self (becoming self-centered) and encourage others to do the same.

These ideas and concepts often create uncertainty and friction for organizational leaders because we are often required to do what our employers want us to do regardless of whether we agree or not. Being an intentional Spiritually Aligned Leader within an organizational context is absolutely attainable and will bring huge success to any leader willing to practice the skills.

# CHAPTER SIX

# ACCEPTANCE
# AND NON-JUDGMENT

The practice of Acceptance and Non-Judgment are critical Tools of Intention for the Spiritually Aligned Leader. As you might imagine Acceptance and Non-Judgment, although different, have an important relationship. Let's begin by considering the value of practicing Non-Judgment.

## Non-Judgment

When was the last time you judged something or someone? When we ask this question in our workshops and seminars we often get the answer, "ten seconds ago." Most of us go through our day judging and assessing everything against our own personal perspective. When I use the term judgment, I am not suggesting that we shouldn't have things we like and dislike. We all have preferences that make us unique and special and allow us to follow our own truth. The concern comes in when we negatively judge another person or situation as being good or bad, right or wrong. We not only judge other people, we also judge ourselves in a negative way. We are often hardest on ourselves.

The noise between our ears can be incredibly detrimental to our well-being unless we cultivate our ability to manage and negotiate with it. The conversations we have with our Roommate/Ego are often based on judgments. We can define Ego as that voice that wants to make us right and someone else wrong, but our Ego can also make us wrong, letting us know that we are not good enough, not deserving, not worthy of abundance and greatness. The Ego plays a significant role in how we feel about ourselves. As you practice becoming the Observer, you will begin to recognize when you are judging yourself and others. Again we ask that you monitor how you feel. It is your key indicator of when things are in alignment and when they are not.

Judgment can be a double-edged sword. Most of us believe that when we judge someone else by saying something negative, or thinking something negative about another person, it makes us feel better, more superior, but this is not true. It may make you feel better for a few moments, however, if you are truly honest with yourself you will determine that this type of thinking and behavior does not serve you in the long run, and it often makes you feel worse. Negative "water cooler" talk at work—those times when people seek out others to validate their dislikes and judgments, does not improve a situation, nor does it make anyone feel better. In the end it only breeds more negativity. Remember that like attracts like. Everything mirrors back at you, so if you want positive results you have to have positive thoughts and feelings. Negative, judgmental thoughts and feelings about others or about situations cannot create positive results.

The same tools and practices pertain to relationships and how you feel about the significant other person in your life. I have been married for over thirty-one years, so I absolutely know about the ups and downs of a long-term relationship. There were times of complete euphoria. There were also many times in those years when circumstances were not great. Many of us feel that we have a right to judge those that are closest to us. This is not true. We absolutely have no right to judge anyone else. When we learn to not harshly judge our partner, life becomes much more balanced and peaceful.

Over the years you will see things in your partner that you don't like. They say something that you know, and often they also know, will upset you. They begin to irritate you and do and say things that just don't align with your values. As we judge what they say and do, we have conversations with our Roommate. We want to be right and we want them to be wrong. We may not do this intentionally or consciously, but we do it. We keep thinking about it and maybe even talk about it with a friend, and then the next time our partner walks into the room we now have the expectation that they will say or do something that we don't like. We build a story in our head about our partner that is negative, judgmental and non-serving. We might even believe we have a right to assist in the directing of our partner's life. If only they did it this way, if only they listened to our good advice. Because we are focused on the wrong things and have begun to build a negative story about our partner, we will see these perceived negative attributes before anything else. If this continues, we end up in argument after argument, followed by silence and more distance.

If you ever find yourself in this situation, you need to do a couple of things very quickly. Become the Observer of your judgments—recognize and own them. Then make a list of all of the reasons you married your partner in the first place. What are the great attributes that attracted you to each other? What do they do well? Every night journal about the good times and the reasons you fell in love with them. Change what you are thinking about by looking for every opportunity to see what you love in your partner. Remember, you only get to lead yourself, not your partner. Spiritually Aligned Leaders completely understand that their job is to lead themselves and let everyone else lead him or herself.

As you create more positive energy thoughts, and you journal about all the things your partner does that you appreciate, you will begin to get perspective. Remember that perceived bad behavior is created and learned. As you create thoughts and feelings that are at a higher vibrational frequency (more positive) then you will be ready to build a plan for yourself. That plan could include honesty before kindness, but remember that your honesty must come with good intentions. If your intention is to improve your relationship, and to be honest with your partner, you will have a much better opportunity for a meaningful conversation. Because you have removed negative judgments, you will be able to share with your partner how you feel, with no negative connection to them. The conversation will be about you, and how you feel, and what you need, instead of what they are doing or not doing. Remember you don't get to determine what is best for them—you only get to do this for yourself.

You may, in the end, determine that you need to leave your partner. It might become clear that you need something very different. You may be unable to find a place in the middle that will allow you to share your unique journeys together without imposing on each other in a negative way. If this is the case and you have done all of the positive work, your transition out of the relationship can be done with balance and perspective instead of anger, frustration and feelings of betrayal. This does not mean that you won't feel sad and experience grief. This is normal and we would never suggest that you try to ignore or suppress your natural feelings. In fact it is the opposite—you recognize your feelings, you accept them and honor them, but you also find ways to move through them quickly. You are able to do this because you have done a lot of the work in advance. You have been intentional and deliberate in a positive way and you did not become reactionary or act on auto-pilot. You did not judge your partner negatively; you accepted and allowed your partner to be him/herself knowing that they are the only one that can lead themselves in alignment with their own truth. You are not responsible for how your partner feels or reacts. You are only responsible for yourself and you will find that your moments of sadness and grief are lessened. It can be very different for a person who has not done this work and who is highly judgmental about their partner. There is usually a lot of negative energy, anger and blaming. This serves no one.

I am sometimes asked about the role that evaluation and judgment plays in the corporate world. Of course evaluation of employees from the leader's perspective is important however, the way in which we do it in most organizations today, impacts most employees in a negative way. I have not met a leader yet that loves performance management. This is because it is not conducive to open, honest dialogue with good intention. It is conducive to judgment, scoring and reward or lack of reward. I believe, the original intent of performance management, was positive. However, like many things within our corporate world, it became another heavily autocratic and bureaucratic process that has lost its original intent and focuses on one person's judgment of another.

Sometimes becoming a Spiritually Aligned Leader means you might feel isolated from others. People's natural tendency to debate, to argue about what is best for family members or for children, creates an environment where your positive energy may not fit. You may find yourself moving away from the drama and negative energy, choosing a different path. This does not mean that you think you are better than someone else and it does not mean that you don't love that other person; it may simply mean that you choose not to be around that person as there is no alignment within your own positive energy. You choose to surround yourself with positive energy and therefore you choose not to spend too much time with those who would judge or make negative comments about others or situations.

You recognize that life is about *free will* and as a result you make intentional and deliberate choices for yourself that are Spiritually Aligned and that come from within. One of the choices I made several years ago was to remove all forms of negative media from my life. As I made a decision not to watch the news, read a newspaper or engage in negative drama within my circles, my world began to change. My life flowed with positive energy. I was able to exponentially increase the positive feelings and positive results that came into my life. It is possible that some of my colleagues found me to be a little reclusive and rigid in my choices. I suspect that on more than one occasion there has been a negative conversation about who I am, and who I have become. It may be a little strange for someone working extensively in the business and corporate world not to read the newspaper, but this practice, (or lack thereof) allows me to do what I do. Each shift was a personal choice and those choices have allowed me to stay in alignment. Spiritually Aligned Leaders often become more selective with the energy (situations, people) they expose themselves to.

Negative judgments that you have about yourself are also very detrimental and affect our choices. If caught up in this kind of thinking, we often make decisions from a position of fear, negativity and a sense of lack. When we focus on what brings us joy and makes us feel great, we can make sound decisions and move in a positive direction.

This does not mean that we should not look at ourselves with curiosity and exploration. It is important that we ask ourselves the hard questions: Why do I seem to do the same things over and over again that do not serve me? Is there something here that I need to deal with? Why do I continually feel a sense of unworthiness? Why do I put others needs in front of my own and then feel resentful?

If you haven't already done so, write out your story and determine whether you want to keep that story (some or all). Consider the influences of others in your life, your upbringing and the judgments of others over the years. Often we judge ourselves, very harshly because we don't believe we are good enough, smart enough, or capable enough. If we are truly honest with ourselves we might also admit that we believe we are not worthy or deserving of happiness and abundance. In most cases a person logically (left-brain/right-brain) will say, "Of course I know I am worthy and deserving of happiness and abundance." But they will then admit that deep down inside they don't *feel* (heart-centered) worthy and deserving. It is one thing to think it—it is completely another to *feel* it. Each of us needs to address these feelings (unworthiness) and understand where they come from. We are all deserving of abundance and there is enough to go around. If we believe that like attracts like and that the world mirrors back to us, then we have to address what we are putting out energetically, through our thoughts, and most importantly our feelings, to attract different results.

The practice of journaling and meditation along with the practice of becoming conscious and present-minded, will help you navigate through your past story to see how it has affected your present beliefs and the conversations you have with yourself about yourself. You can then create a new story based on your internal truth, your true essence.

## No One in Front or Behind

Organizational leaders, parents, teachers, politicians, and individual community contributors—we all need to learn a very simple truth. No one is in front of us; no one is behind us. We all walk beside each other. Unfortunately many of us still live in an old world order that puts levels and hierarchies in everything we do. We place parents, teachers, doctors, politicians and anyone else that comes into our lives ahead of us or behind us in the pecking order of life.

I would love to know who created this pecking order as it makes no sense and is absolutely not Spiritually Aligned thinking. Full and complete non-judgment and acceptance of others allows us to ensure that we never put anyone in front of us or behind us. There will never be anyone better or worse than you. We are all truly equal and as you begin to feel and internalize this belief and practice, you will become highly effective at whatever role you play. That does not mean that there is no bad behavior. Most of us would agree that there is bad behavior in the world or less than desirable behavior, but remember that behavior is learned. We are not born with bad behavior. The behavior may not be in alignment with your truth however it is the behavior not the person.

The teacher is not better than any of their students. The teacher simply plays a different role and is at a different stage in life than the student. Consider two teachers in your life. The teacher who absolutely believed everyone was equal and were all there to learn from each other, compared with the teacher who made it very clear that they were superior, and in complete authority. Which teacher put out more positive energy? Who created a better learning environment? Which one was more effective in actually teaching?

Now consider the business leader who truly emulates humility, consistency and sees himself or herself as equal to everyone else, regardless of title, pay or organizational level. Compare this to the leader who implies they know more, are better suited to make decisions and who clearly puts themselves above those they lead. Which leader gets more engagement, more commitment, more flow of knowledge, skills and ability? We intuitively know that it is not about who signs the check or makes the final decisions. It is about the energy and environment the leader creates through their own beliefs about equality, acceptance and non-judgment that create highly effective and productive work environments.

The parent who does not think they have all the answers for the child and who accepts each child as a unique individual with no judgment, is more likely to create a positive environment where the child will feel heard, accepted and honored for who they are. The parent is accepting of the fact that parenting is a crapshoot at best, and they, the parents, have as much to learn from the child as the child can learn from the parents. The parent does not judge the child, but seeks to understand the child.

## Acceptance

Questions are the most important part of learning a new practice or in this case, Tools of Intention. When teaching the Creating Positive Energy workshops, we often show a picture (I love visuals) of a very small ant pushing a massive boulder up a large hill and we ask our clients if they have ever felt like the ant. I think that most of us have experienced that feeling of overwhelm, when we are trying to change something in our lives that just doesn't seem to want to budge.

Unfortunately we still live in a society that teaches us from a young age, that if we want something, we have to work hard for it and that anything worth having is worth working for. This belief can create an environment where a person fixates on what they desire and then works relentlessly to get it. But what happens when life is not cooperating, when things just don't seem to be lining up, or when someone is not doing what we think they should? We try to change the situation. We employ new tactics in pursuit of our goal and we try to influence another person to see things our way. When they don't, we lament that things would be easier if we all just agreed. We keep pushing the boulder until we are frustrated and exhausted and sometimes the boulder rolls right over us. Many of us stubbornly return to pushing the boulder again and again but becoming aware means we stop trying to change *what is*.

If you find yourself in a situation like this it helps to first practice becoming The Observer and ask yourself, "Does the situation I am trying to change directly involve my life?" Most often the things we are trying to influence or change concern someone else's life. Then ask yourself another important question: Why am I doing this? If you are truly honest with yourself you will admit that your Ego is in the way.

In business we often try to influence people to see a situation or problem the way that we see the problem. Now granted, it is important to share your opinions on subject matters where you have expertise. In a business context, you are often paid for your intellect, knowledge, experience and education and you are expected to provide your professional opinion on topics. When a colleague has a different opinion on how to solve a problem, we feel it is our duty, our obligation, to show them our way. This is not a bad thing. It only becomes a bad thing when you start to push the boulder up the hill. You might decide to share your opinion a couple of times or you might find a new way to rephrase your insights, but once you have done this it is very important that you step back and accept whatever decision is made, especially if the decision differs from your perspective.

I have worked with and coached many middle and senior managers, who have derailed themselves specifically because they were unable to let go of an issue at work. They were pushing a large boulder up a hill and, getting nowhere, except drawing a lot of attention to themselves unnecessarily. I would suggest that most of us have done this before and that most of this behavior is fueled by our Ego, or Roommate, that voice in our head that has convinced us that we are right and others are wrong and that those involved need to hear what we have to say. We lose perspective. We get focused on shifting the views of others.

This behavior often stems from our societal norms and institutions that say there is a right way and there is a wrong way; situations are either good or bad. Many of us still live in a world that promotes a win/lose mentality, but it is the intertwined values of Acceptance and Non-Judgment that allow us to become significantly more balanced and at peace—to truly "win." In the context of work, it is important for us to recognize that once we have shared our views, based on what we know through our experience and education, our job is to let go and allow things to unfold. We are not paid to push boulders up hills. Acceptance is an intentional choice that allows us to let go early and to move forward with integrity and focus. A Spiritually Aligned Leader practices acceptance and understanding to arrive at a place of heart-centered execution.

When things do not go our way it does not mean that we are wrong or that we lost. It simply means things have gone in a different direction. *It is what it is.* Once this happens our role is to accept and support. You don't have to agree in order to accept.

You can absolutely disagree with a decision and still be in a place of acceptance. You are right from your own perspective and within organizational life there will always be someone who makes the final decision.

When we accept and seek to understand we can lead in a very different way. We are able to release our Ego and the chatter with our Roommate and simply move forward with ease. Consider this important statement—you can choose to be happy or you can choose to be right. It is absolutely a choice and the choice is based on acceptance or the stubborn refusal not to accept.

It is important to note that acceptance does not mean that you become a doormat, with no opinion and no voice. It means that you accept what you cannot change. Leaders need to monitor how they feel and make sure that, while they are accepting of things they cannot change, they feel good about their acceptance, knowing it is the right thing to do. A feeling of relief often accompanies acceptance; one is no longer pushing the boulder. If you truly do not *feel* good then call in the Observer and ask yourself the hard questions: Does this decision that is about to be made violate my personal truth, what I know to be true (right) for me? Will it place me out of alignment? If you cannot support this decision and feel good about it, then you have to make a different choice. Organizational leaders who are Spiritually Aligned understand the difference between a simple business decision that does not go in the direction they feel it should, versus a decision that violates their values, truth and alignment.

In the corporate context we often take things very seriously when it is not necessary to do so. This intense need to be right and to have things move in a specific direction is very counter-productive and requires significant amount of energy from the leader. The Spiritually Aligned Leader does their homework, understands the situation, presents the information based on all of the data available, including the right-brain and the heart-center (intuition) and then lets go. This ability to let go and accept within the work context is critical.

If you work in an environment where you are required to do things over and over again that do not align with your truth or if you feel that you don't fit within the value system of the organization or department, then different considerations need to be made. Here is an example of what we might hear when working with a client who has these concerns, "I work for a micromanaging leader who will not allow me to make any decisions. There is no collaboration, no inclusion; simply orders that are expected to be followed with no consideration of outcomes or impacts on others. I am drowning and feel completely sick about it." We would never tell this client to quit their job or simply leave. Running is never the answer. Spiritually Aligned Leaders are intentional and deliberate in everything they do and they absolutely believe and know that they are responsible for their outcomes. They recognize the importance and need to keep their own personal power, to monitor how they feel and build a strategy that allows them to move forward in a positive way.

How the client feels is extremely important. Their feelings are based on what they have been thinking about as it relates to this manager, so the first thing the client needs to note is what they think about their manager on a daily basis. We suggest the simple practice of writing down one thing every night that their leader does really well. This can be tough to begin with, especially if the person has been unhappy for a long time. Start with the obvious. "My boss makes sure I get paid on time each month." Some other positive attributes include. "My boss is great at executing the corporate strategies." "My boss ensures that I have the things I need to do my job." "My boss approves my vacation time each summer."

These are small examples, but it is critical that we shift what we think about if we want to shift how we feel. Now you might be thinking, *how does changing what I think about change my boss's micromanaging behavior?* It probably won't, but that is not your concern; your concern must be how you feel about your situation. Remember, if all you think about is the fact that your boss is a micromanager and you really don't like or respect him, every time he walks into a room and says something, all you will see and hear is the micromanaging person that you don't respect. Your view of this person is not balanced, positive or constructive in any way. Your view is negative, low energy and not Spiritually Aligned, so you need to change what you think about so that you can change how you feel.

This does not mean that you need to stay working for this person forever, but it does mean that how you deal with this issue actually lies within you, not within the micromanager. Your manager has his own stuff to deal with. He is on his own journey, growing his own Tree of Abundance and making his own choices about life, work, and family. He may not be a Spiritually Aligned Leader. He may rely more heavily on left-brain and auto-pilot than on a balanced approach that includes the right-brain and heart-center, but what does how he behaves have to do with you and how can you change this? It has nothing to do with you–it's not your job. Your job is to apply the Tools of Intention so that *you* can become a balanced leader who leads self from the inside out in an intentional and deliberate way. When you do this, things always work out. You feel centered, at peace and accepting of how things are. You also empower yourself instead of relying on others to empower you. Life becomes easy and you stop pushing boulders.

As you work on this long list of things your boss does really well, you will begin to remind yourself that your boss is a person too, a person who has his own issues and challenges that he is working through. You don't have any real idea what he deals with on a day-to-day basis. If you believe that all people are born good at heart with good intentions then you can take an even broader view. Most people are not born behaving badly. Bad behavior is learned through situation and life experiences and most of us have no idea what our boss or manager has been through in their life. You may say, "but this does not give them the right to be disrespectful or non-inclusive," but remember YOU feel this way. You have the choice to control what you think about and the conversations you have with your Roommate. You can have negative thoughts that do not serve you and make you feel badly or you can change what you think about. Also note, that what you think about does not affect your manager, it only affects you, so change what you think about and you will begin to change how you feel. As you change how you feel, you will begin to get perspective, which will assist you in making the next decisions.

You might discover that your boss is not that bad after all and that what you needed was to see things from a more balanced approach. However, you might also see that although you are feeling better and have gained acceptance of the situation you would still like to make a change. Now, here is the great part. When you go to make a change you do so with positive energy. You make a change with the real you, the Spiritually Aligned you, at the helm. You have a balanced perspective that allows you to build a solid plan that aligns with what you want. You are not running to the next job or company, you are not running from a bad situation, blaming your manager, simply to escape. You have created positive energy around yourself and you have decided to see the good in your boss, to work constructively with the team and as you do this you can build a plan to leave on your terms. When you put a positive intention out into the world, one that is fueled by positive energy and great feelings, you will have amazing results.

You can leave the organization on your terms, in a positive way. You leave as a Spiritually Aligned Leader who absolutely knew what he or she wanted, and directed an intentional plan based on positivity and great energy. This is what being a Spiritually Aligned Leader is all about. No negative thoughts or negative energy surrounding your boss, you or your organization. You are not a victim. You make everything about you and what you want. You focus on and align to your highest intentions.

Boulder pushing does not work and will usually create negative energy, thoughts and feelings. Sharing your thoughts, intellect and experience in a positive and constructive way through honesty and confidence (not Ego) with the ability to accept and let go is Spiritually Aligned.

Regardless of the role we play, or the stage we are at in our lives, when we practice consistently, and live intentionally with the belief that no one should ever be put in front of us or behind us, we can become highly effective. We encourage everyone around us to seek their greatness for themselves and that they need to honor their gifts and abilities.

When we put someone ahead of us or look up to them and think they are better or more skilled, we immediately put that relationship at risk. Eventually they will let us down because we can never be in complete alignment with another person. Their truth and passion is their's and your truth and passion is yours. They will never fully align with you or your needs. You should not want to be like someone else. You need to go inside and create your own truth and greatness; find your uniqueness, nurture and grow your own tree and allow others to do the same without judgment. You are never better or worse than another person, you are simply different. The greatest gift we can give to ourselves is acceptance, non-judgment and the willingness to find and pursue our unique passion, joy and gifts to serve the world.

.

# CHAPTER SEVEN

# FORGIVENESS

The act of forgiveness is a fundamental tool for the Spiritually Aligned Leader. We have all been wronged at some time or felt that we have been betrayed or disrespected. Some people's stories include very sad and horrific past wrongdoings that make it incredibly difficult for them to forgive, and yet forgiveness is fundamental for parents, leaders and organizations as a whole.

In our coaching practice we have had the opportunity to work with many people from all industries, age groups and cultures. Through these encounters we have met some amazing and very interesting people. For the purposes of this chapter, I will refer to two examples that stand out.

Sandra was a beautiful, tall and very confident woman who I only met twice. Sandra had a couple of specific things she wanted to work on which were unrelated to her relationship with her dad. However, during our first meeting she mentioned her dad several times and I could tell that she was harboring significant negative energy around this relationship. As our conversation progressed, she informed me that her deceased father was very abusive and he had passed away when she was nineteen. For many years, family and friends had told her that she should try to find a way to forgive him. In fact, in the past she ended up seeking the advice of a spiritual medium in an effort to understand her feelings around this relationship. I believe that she eventually convinced herself that this old relationship had no impact on her present life. She believed that she had released any negative feelings and was *over it*. She told me this during both of our meetings. I wondered, *why did he continue to creep into our conversations if she had released her negative feelings*. It was clear to me that there was way more to this then she originally described.

When we had an opportunity to discuss the concepts of forgiveness she simply said, "I will never forgive him for what he did." What is interesting about this story is that her father had been dead for over eighteen years. In my mind she was clearly stuck. I believe it was her unwillingness to consider forgiveness that was holding her back. When I asked her specific questions around forgiveness, she was relentless in her position; she did not need to forgive her father and that forgiveness would not help her move forward. We did not work together very long and I have no idea whether she found a way to forgive and move forward.

Another client, a mid-level manager in a large organization, came to us for some coaching and discovered quickly that forgiveness was fundamental to his ability to move on and create the career and work-life that he truly wanted. Steve had worked for a large organization for over twenty-two years. The Vice-President, in the area in which he worked, had personally asked him to take a lateral management position to assist the company with a very challenging situation. Steve had been called upon in the past to assist the corporation and each time he had agreed. Steve knew the department in question and he was not really interested in this opportunity. The work itself was not something Steve felt was challenging and he knew the department had lots of systemic issues. He wanted the Vice-President to know that he would take this new lateral role, and help the company out, but that he wanted to be considered, for the next director position. A straightforward and candid individual, Steve came right out and told the Vice-President that he was very interested in a Director role (promotion) and felt that he was ready. The Vice-President agreed that he would consider Steve for a future promotion and so Steve accepted the assignment even though the work was not appealing.

Steve worked in this new role for about eighteen months fixing the problems and performing as expected by his boss. As a very driven and accomplished leader, Steve was ready to get the next promotion. He felt he had done everything right and was absolutely shocked, angered and frustrated when the director position he had been working toward was given to another leader. He was not even asked to apply. The anger that Steve felt toward his organization was very strong, and he began to disengage. Steve, who had been a high performing leader in the past, was now a disengaged manager who felt great resentment toward his organization. He began to look outside the company for employment.

Had Steve not worked on forgiveness, the Vice-President would have lost a great leader, Steve would have lost his fabulous tenure with the organization, and the company would have lost some long-term intellectual property.

Two things occurred for Steve, during our coaching work, which were pivotal in his journey to becoming a Spiritually Aligned Leader. Before agreeing to take the lateral position, Steve was in a role that he absolutely loved. It was challenging, he was working with great people, had tons of autonomy and was valued as a key contributor. So why would he leave and go to the new lateral management position that he knew he didn't want? When I asked him why he took the position he said, "Because they were willing to consider me for the next promotion." Then I asked, "When they initially came to you with the proposal, did they mention you would be given the next director role?" Steve answered, "No I was the one that brought it up."

It's possible the Vice-President said what Steve wanted to hear in an effort to get Steve to agree to help him out, but what's more important, is the fact that Steve allowed his Ego to make his decisions, not his heart. Steve knew from the beginning that he didn't want the role, but he decided that if he could get the Director's position in a year or two it was worth it. By settling for the needs of the Ego, Steve became completely attached to the idea that he would be the next director, but of course when the time came, Steve was overlooked.

As we talked further, Steve could clearly recall knowing inside that the role was not a good fit for him and that he really didn't want it. The result of not listening to that intuitive heart-centered inner voice was that he was stuck doing work he really didn't enjoy.

There are two main reasons why situations like Steve's continue to occur in organizational life. The first is that leaders and managers are not in alignment. The senior leaders dictate the organizational alignment, and it stands to follow that when they are not in alignment, the organization cannot be either. The second reason is best illustrated by what happened when I asked Steve why he wanted the specific director position. He couldn't give a definite answer as to why that position was so important. In our work together he was honest enough to admit that it was not the role and the specific work that attracted him, but the title. We know what is at play in these scenarios—Ego. The Vice-President was also not in alignment because he was not in a position to lead Steve to believe that he would be considered for the Director position. He could not have known what the future would hold and therefore if he had been completely honest with Steve, he would have told him this. His Ego was also at play, working to solve a problem in the quickest and easiest way, even if it meant misalignment.

As I continued to work with Steve and ask him questions, he realized that first he needed to forgive himself for not listening to that inner voice, and then he needed to forgive the Vice-President. Steve invited that situation into his life and had to take ownership of it if he was going to move on successfully. Steve realized that he was now disengaged from work, not aligned with either himself or his organization, and that people around him knew it. Steve's next task was to go inside and truly listen for the answers. One of the answers was to recognize and take responsibility for the situation and the second was to forgive and let go. This would be the beginning of his ability to move on and make better choices for himself and for the organization.

Organizations need engaged and Spiritually Aligned Leaders who listen to their internal guidance and who are not afraid to act on that information. Leaders and employees need to do work that is in alignment with their interests, passions and organizational goals. Steve was able to tap into the Tools of Intention by first observing the negative thoughts he had and the negative feelings they were creating. Then he had to accept things the way they were. Negatively judging his boss for the way things transpired did not serve Steve in any way and so he needed to monitor and observe his judgments and make different choices. Once he did this he could begin to forgive both himself and the Vice-President.

As Steve began to forgive the Vice-President, he was now in

a position to consider what he had learned through this event. Could he actually turn his anger to forgiveness and his forgiveness into gratitude? Could he become grateful to the Vice-President for teaching him this fabulous lesson about Ego?

### It's Not About the Perpetrator

There seems to be a common belief that forgiveness is about the perpetrator, and that the victim needs to find a way to make what happened okay. Nothing could be further from the truth. Most people will never forget and completely let go of the damages created by a very negative relationship. However, in the right context, we can find ways to shift the energy around these events to one of healing and personal transformation. The events can become catalysts that propel us forward in a positive way.

First we need to understand that the act of forgiveness heals and frees the person who does the forgiving; the focus is within and not necessarily on the perpetrator. Although my coaching client believed that she had completely dealt with her feelings about her relationship with her father, it was clear that this was still at the root of her unhappiness. She needed to realize that forgiveness has nothing to do with her father and everything to do with her being able to let go and move on. I believe that as a person becomes a Spiritually Aligned Leader, they can let go and forgive. In this way they can turn the negative energy into positive energy and use it to their advantage. I will share a couple of personal stories in an effort to explain in more detail how this can work.

As I have mentioned before, while growing up I was reminded daily that I was overweight and due to events in my childhood, I also felt that I was stupid and never really going to amount to anything. I truly did not love myself and felt lost for many years. Eventually I came to understand that I needed to deal with my past, in particular my relationship with my mom and dad. I needed to forgive and find a way to move on. Through my own experience and witnessing those of my clients, I've come to believe that the most significant shifts in our lives are borne out of forgiveness and if we can shift the forgiveness to gratitude we can truly let go.

I left home with lots of emotional baggage and self-worth issues, although I don't think I could have articulated it back then. I am not sure I knew how unhappy I really was until it began to manifest in other ways later in life. I think many young people leave home with similar feelings. What is really strange about this is that I believe my five siblings and I left home believing that we had this great family life, full of harmony and love. None of us were truly honest with ourselves, at least I certainly wasn't, and it took me many years later to actually come to terms with why I felt lost and unworthy. Although we were trained to debate and to win, there was this strange belief that we were respectful and compassionate. Nothing could be further from the truth. I now know I was lying to myself because this is what we were taught to believe. My mom would continually state what a great family we had, that we were so lucky to have these relationships, and how successful and independent we had all become. The question was, were we happy? Did we have healthy relationships with each other and with our parents? My dad had single-handedly created children who were competitive, assertive and had extremely poor listening skills. As grown adults we were still trying to win his love that, by his own admission, he would never share. I tried to tell myself that I was loved and that he was just emotionally withdrawn.

Early on in my adult life, I started to go inside and ask the hard questions about self-worth and who I was. What I realized over time, and through lots of personal work, was that I had to find a way to forgive and try to release some of my negative feelings (energy). I had felt for many years that I truly was the black sheep of the family and that I had never fit in. I felt that way for most of my life and never really did understand it until my mother revealed one of her "secrets."

I happened to live a long distance from my parents and, as a result, I did not see them very often. One summer in the late 80s I was visiting them at their home. All of my siblings were grown and had moved away. I was now twenty-eight years old with two children and a third one on the way. It was the middle of the summer, a time when some of my siblings would visit with their children. I was five months pregnant and spent most of my time running after a three year old and two year old. Mom and I were in the kitchen one day, doing the dishes, and mom decided to tell me the story about the time she found out she was pregnant with me.

*I couldn't believe I was pregnant again. I already had four children. I had finally lost weight and was feeling good. I was sick about the idea of being pregnant again. I didn't want you and could not believe that I was once again expecting. In those days there were no contraceptives and no way of avoiding it and so there I was expecting again. I spent the entire pregnancy feeling that this was just not fair and when it came time for the delivery I was still feeling really horrible about it. I did not want to take you home. The doctor who delivered you had three sons of his own and so when you arrived, a girl, I asked if he would like a daughter and that I would be happy to give you away.*

My mom finished the story with, "*you were probably eighteen months to two years old before I decided it was okay to have you. It took a long time.*"

Well what do you say to that? How do you respond? I don't remember what I said, but I remember feeling devastated by her words.

Moments like this never completely leave you and sometimes they can act as signposts. At the time I could not see the importance of this conversation but, as the years passed, I worked through my old story, and began to create a new one. I grew curious. Why did my mother tell me this? In the early years following this event I thought it was mean-spirited of her and I think the average person might agree. However, I realized that this story was one of the greatest gifts my mother could have given me. I can't imagine how she felt all those years later, knowing that she never wanted me. She must have intuitively known how it affected me. As time passed I acknowledged that my feelings of not being loved were in fact real and that I had not imagined it, that while in the womb and for the first few years after being born, I had lived in the shadow of her negative feelings about me.

I became aware of a second significant signpost about twenty years after my mother had shared that story with me. When my mom and dad needed to leave their family home, due to illness, one of my sisters was going through their things and came across a portrait of a beautiful woman. She had never seen the picture before and had no idea who the person in the picture was. When she asked my dad about it, the answer was, "I only had one girlfriend other than your mother and this is a picture of her. I dated her in Australia before leaving. Her name was Yvonne."

So not only was I unwanted in those early years; I was named after my father's only girlfriend. Weird! Everything began to make sense. All of the pieces of the puzzle were beginning to come together. I was able to put into context the reason I always felt different, isolated, unloved. My mother gave me the gift of honesty and that is something I regard highly. She did not tell me the truth to hurt me, but as a way for me to understand why I felt the way I felt. I now had a choice as to what I did with those feelings. I could choose to forgive and feel better or remain stuck, feeling unwanted and unloved. I wanted to feel better and this meant that I had to change my thoughts so I could change how I felt.

Forgiveness brings amazing gifts to the forgiver; relief that could never be felt without a full and complete understanding of the intense value of forgiveness. You have to be willing to look for the signs. You have to monitor your thoughts around these negative situations and ask yourself: Are my thoughts good feeling thoughts? Do my thoughts serve me in a positive way? As I asked myself these questions, it became clear I needed to find a way to change my thoughts.

The ways in which my relationship with my father has transformed is of equal significance. I had spent most of my adult life trying to be everything my dad wasn't. I write this now with no negativity, ego or sadness in my heart. In fact I write this with extreme love and gratitude. My dad was competitive, lacked compassion, was argumentative and extremely hard on people. I wanted to be compassionate, loving and accepting of everyone and everything without judgment or ego. That was who I was meant to be; my true nature, my alignment. I became very comfortable and in fact happy to be the black sheep in the family; I didn't need to seek my dad's love to feel self-worth. I set out on a quest to love myself no matter what and to spread that love in every contact I had with my clients, family and friends. Through this I began to really thank my dad for all that he taught me. He was a signpost in my life. His values and choices pointed in one direction and I chose the other; neither one being right or wrong, but simply different. He was the contrast I needed to help define my path. He provided me the opportunity to know who I wanted to be, by knowing whom I didn't want to be. Through this I began to love my dad very much and created a very healthy and loving relationship with him. I also learned empathy and complete acceptance for who he was with no judgment, or negative emotions attached. Anger and sadness turns to forgiveness first, and eventually if you practice the Tools of Intention you move from forgiveness to gratitude.

My dad continues to be a very opinionated, stubborn and assertive person. Our views of life and love are extremely different and he does not believe in any of the things that are in this book. He has stated to me many times that any type of spirituality would never work for him. *He is a man of science and he came from the dirt and is going back to the dirt.* There is nothing more to life and death. I believe that we are spiritual beings having a human experience and we are far more complicated than simply water and carbon. I also absolutely respect that that is how he feels and what he believes in.

Over the years I realized that the contrast between my dad and my true nature was the driving force in my career choices, beliefs and who I ultimately have become. I also believe that the gift of honesty that my mother provided was a significant catalyst in assisting me to detach from an old story and able to create a new story. Through both of these relationships I was able to truly learn to love myself from the inside out. These days I recognize the huge value my relationships with both parents provided and I am grateful for both of these transformational opportunities.

## Compassion

The woman who could not forgive her father for his abusive conduct does not hurt her father, but will continue to be hurt and hold herself back. We clearly know that forgiveness will never make what the person did right. Forgiveness allows a (potential) victim to decide, independently, what they want to do with the negative conversations that take place with the Roommate and the resulting feelings that occur. Do I want to be angry forever? Why do I still feel unworthy? When will I feel completely and totally loving and accepting of myself? All of these questions can only be answered when a person forgives and allows him or herself to move to the next stage of personal acceptance.

A secondary result of forgiveness is often compassion. The victim begins to have compassion for the perpetrator. The person begins to have empathy for the individual who participated in the wrongdoing. The person imagines the pain and sorrow felt by the perpetrator and begins to try to put themselves in the perpetrators' shoes. This is where true compassion comes from. We begin to see how acceptance and forgiveness can occur once we have become the Observer of our thoughts and feelings and we begin to make different choices.

We can practice being present-minded, and conscious and use journaling to allow a means of processing. Meditation and reading inspiring materials to help support our journey to forgiveness and ultimately to becoming Spiritually Aligned Leaders of ourselves are also important practices.

# CHAPTER EIGHT

# DETACHMENT AND UNCONDITIONAL LOVE

Applying the tool of detachment and unconditional love continues to be the hardest skill I practice each day. It requires discipline and a knowing that this is exactly how life is supposed to be. We are supposed to detach so that we can experience unconditional love, but most of us spend so much time worrying about others, and having opinions and views of how others should conduct themselves, that it becomes impossible. Unconditional love is that true love that arises as a result of absolutely accepting, and loving others exactly the way they are. In this place we have no negative feelings, judgments or thoughts of, "if only they would…" Detachment allows us to find that sweet spot of true unconditional love that creates an empowering level of freedom.

Detachment can be applied in several ways, and for the purposes of our Tools of Intention, I will share the two most common ways. The first is that of detaching from what others believe, feel and do. The second application is the ability to detach from how and when results manifest in your life. Let's explore the application of detachment from what others believe, feel and do first.

### Detaching from Others—A Personal Story

We all have hidden expectations of others. We want the best for our children, family and friends, and as a result we have opinions about how they should go about their lives. We see their life through our eyes. For example, we truly believe that we unconditionally love our children, but often there are unspoken conditions to our love—they are subtle and yet they restrict our relationships. Of course, our intentions are good, but this is where the problem lies. Why do we feel we have a right to an opinion about how others choose their path? Everyone is on his or her own unique journey. Our focus must be on our journey and no one else's.

In Chapter Three I wrote about my son, Scott, and how he was so sick for what seemed to be a very long time. Every day I worried and I believed that he was making many poor decisions. I wanted him to leave his girlfriend and I desperately wanted my old Scott back. Remember my phone conversation with the clinic, when the Doctor told me that I should prepare for the worst, and that I needed to accept that I might have lost him already? Well, shortly after this, the family (minus Scott) attended one of our regular family counseling sessions. We were desperately trying to come to terms with what was going on. I felt like I had been pushing a massive boulder up a hill for over twelve months. I was tired and exhausted trying to get back to where we had once been as a family—united, connected and positively engaged in each other's activities. At this specific session, something happened that is hard to describe, but to this day I believe was a turning point in what seemed like a never-ending nightmare.

The session unfolded in the usual way as we tearfully expressed our fears, how much we missed Scott and how much we wanted our old life and relationships back. I am not sure how it happened, but almost at the exact same time, each of us came to a place of equanimity and release—we let go. We detached from the outcome and in that moment, we each found unconditional love for Scott and for each other. I cannot describe how we got there, maybe the angels were helping us along, but Geoff, Mike, Bob and I, all in our own way, came to the same realization. We needed to find our own truth, to seek alignment, and to stop trying to get Scott to live the life that we wanted him to live. We realized that we needed to accept that Scott was on his own journey, (creating his own tree; such as it was) and it was time that we got out of his journey, and allowed him to find his own way, whatever that meant. We had to stop climbing his tree. It was not our place to have influence on Scott's choices or how his journey unfolded.

Many would say that Scott was very self-destructive, and maybe he was, but what I needed to do was ask myself over and over again was "What did it have to do with me?" In these moments of detachment I found an unconditional love for my son. I realized that each of us had made Scott's situation about *us*. We internalized everything that happened that year. It was personal. It was all about how I felt, and my perception about what he was doing to our family. I made Scott's choices about me. Scott was on a unique journey to find himself and although it seemed to us a self-destructive path, the truth was it didn't have anything to do with us. We would never experience that year the way Scott did and we would never truly understand what he was going through.

This discovery allowed me to understand my true role, which was to love Scott regardless of his choices or the journey he was on. I needed to be there for him, if or when he ever wanted to rejoin the family, but it was not my place to interfere with his journey. I'd been the small little ant pushing a massive boulder up a hill and neither the boulder nor the hill was mine. Detachment allowed me to accept and move on.

I quickly learned that Scott needed to find his own way out and that we needed to be there if and when he ever decided to do so. Otherwise it was not my journey nor was it my path. I had the ability to choose my thoughts and the resulting feelings and emotions that they invoked. I chose to let go and move forward with positive thoughts and to remove the negative feelings I had been living with for more than a year. I was finally managing my Ego in a positive and productive way. My thoughts became about how much I loved Scott and what an amazing person he was, and how when he came through this he would be able to truly own his own recovery and journey. It would finally be his life and no one else's.

I never spoke to my husband or other two children about my revelation; however I didn't need to because they all seemed to find their own way on the path to detachment and unconditional love. The freedom and joy that comes from truly understanding unconditional love is like nothing else you have ever experienced. I believe it is the freedom we all seek. The complete and total acceptance and detachment from those we truly love makes room for a relationship that is full of acceptance, joy and peace and unconditional love. It is powerful beyond measure.

I am challenged all the time when I tell this story while teaching how to detach from your views of how others should live their lives. I have had mothers speak out about their children who are addicted to drugs or living on the street. My comments are always the same. "How is trying to change things working for you? Are you getting great results with the other person? What are the dominant thoughts you have each day about this situation? Do you feel good, with corresponding emotions? How is this pushing of a boulder that is not yours to push affecting the other relationships in your life?"

I speak from experience. There were many times when I was completely desperate and wanted to save Scott (rob him from his own life choices) and take him away from everything. I even thought about kidnapping him and getting him on a plane and away from the influences of those I thought were negatively impacting his life. Scott was on his own journey, and if he could find his own way out he would always own his recovery. He would be stronger, self-reliant and much more resilient moving forward.

My job was to get back into alignment with my own truth. I could begin to feel joy again, even though nothing had changed with Scott. I also know now that the only way to ever have organic influence on those around you is to lead-self and practice the Tools of Intention every day.

The more I detached from Scott and his choices, the more I loved him. It was the most amazing experience I have ever had and to this day I am so thankful for the gift that Scott provided us. I sometimes wonder if the journey we were on, during this time, was exactly what we needed to evolve and expand in our own spiritual growth. I apply what I learned through this every day in my business and personal life. It is the foundation of Spiritually Aligned Leadership.

Shortly after our newfound Spiritual Alignment, something miraculous happened. Maybe it was a reward for being open to evolution and seeking unconditional love, or just maybe the world was mirroring back at us. *Like attracts like.* Within six weeks of our personal evolution, Scott came home and said, "I am going skydiving." I was shocked. We really hadn't spoken in months and

Scott was not accustomed to telling me what he was doing. We rarely saw Scott and now he was announcing a skydiving adventure.

Scott is very handsome. As an adult he has always had a full head of dark brown hair with a well-manicured beard and mustache. When Scott was a young child, people would stop us in a shopping mall and say, "wow what a beautiful baby, he is gorgeous." As Scott grew up he was noticed wherever he went, for having a pleasant and welcoming appeal. Two days after Scott announced the skydiving adventure, he arrived home and there wasn't a hair anywhere on his head. He had shaved his entire head of hair, as well as his beard. We were all in shock. I had to monitor my internal dialogue very carefully over the coming days. You can imagine how easy it could have become to let my thoughts run amuck. I would not allow my Ego to come in and start creating stories that weren't real.

Three days later, Scott jumped out of a plane and then immediately asked if the whole family would watch the video of his adventure. Again, we were shocked. Within one week we went from not having much of a relationship, to being asked to watch a video with him. This might not seem like a big deal, but to us it was a huge step. We hadn't watched anything as a family in over seven months. I can clearly remember this moment; the entire family for the first times in so long all hovering around the computer screen watching him jump out of a plane, 3000 feet in the air. The jump was set to one of Scott's favorite Coldplay songs and it gave me chills.

One week later, Scott announced he was moving to Victoria, BC. He had been in discussion with his cousin and they had decided to take an apartment together. WOW. Things were moving unbelievably fast, but we were detached, loving, and simply watching as Scott made each decision. Within three weeks of skydiving we were saying good-bye to Scott at the airport. He was leaving the life that had caused him so much pain and was moving on to a new chapter. With an emotional and yet joyful good-bye, we left him at the security gate. When I got home I went into Scott's room, and noticed on the dresser his prescription for the anti-depressants. I called him immediately to let him know, and his response was simply, "I don't need them anymore; I have been off them for over four weeks."

Scott is now doing great, loving his new life and his new relationships are full of joy and abundance. Our relationships with all three of our children are completely different because of this experience. We were able to truly experience unconditional love through practicing detachment, and as a result we now apply this to each of our relationships with family and others.

The freedom that you experience when you get out of another person's journey, especially your children's, is so powerful. Our ability to truly love from a non-ego based position of detachment creates a love that is empowering and freeing. Each person is on his or her own journey of discovery and evolution and our only role is to love unconditionally, especially when a person we care about makes decisions that we might not make for ourselves. Our choices are ours alone, and we are here to lead-self and not to lead others. We need to get back into our own journey and leave others to explore and seek their own true journey. Grow and nurture your own tree and stop trying to climb someone else's.

### Detachment in the Workplace

At work, leaders can benefit dramatically from detaching from the results of employees. This doesn't mean that they don't care, or that they do not manage performance. In fact, it means the opposite. When the leader is heavily attached to *how* an employee performs their duties, the manager will often make comparison or give feedback that tells the employee they are not good enough. Emotions get in the way and the messaging is poor. When the leader detaches from the actions of employees, they are able to have the important conversations regarding how the employee feels about their contribution. The leader can truly make it about the employee, instead of making it about themselves, and the impact of the employee's work on the leader or the department. Detaching emotionally, and realizing that each person and every employee wants to be in control of his or her own performance and measurements, allows the leader to become Spiritually Aligned. The leader asks the right questions, encourages the employee to find their own truth and to be honest with themselves in a way that assists the employee in leading themselves and becoming Spiritually Aligned. Detachment is a critical tool for the Spiritually Aligned organizational Leader. We will discuss this further in Chapter Eleven.

The other side of this intentional tool is the ability to detach from what others think or feel about you. Many of us spend a significant amount of time thinking and worrying about whether we make others happy; whether we meet their expectations. Many of our coaching clients believe that they are not trying to make others happy, but as we ask questions, and they explore their feelings, they discover that at the core of their concerns, are their attempts at trying to meet others' expectations. The issues they are dealing with have less to do with them, and more to do with pleasing others. This of course comes full circle and has everything to do with them and the conversations they are having with the Roommate.

Most of us are somewhat curious about how we are perceived by others and we wonder whether we would be happy knowing more about how others see us. How others perceive you is only important from one perspective, it allows you to decide whether there is anything in your behavior that you would like to change. You can ask yourself some candid and valuable questions: Does that person's perception matter to me? What might it be based on? Do I want to change something I am doing? This is the only value this information brings. Using this information, especially for leaders in organizational life, gives you the ability to decide if you want to make changes.

If you want to know what others think, ask them to provide you feedback in a candid way with good intentions. Then evaluate the information you get, and determine for yourself if there is merit in making any changes. However, only make a change if what you learn highlights a blind-spot; something you did not know about yourself before, and you determine that you would be happier and closer to your true alignment if you made the change. If you are upset at the feedback you receive, ask yourself why. If you don't feel good, that means that there is something there you need to address.

Guilt is another emotion that has no place in our lives. It is the one emotion that serves no purpose and needs to be monitored and observed carefully. When a person does something out of guilt or out of a need to make another person happy, the results are often more negative emotions such as resentment and frustration. We all have experienced guilt and have done something only because someone else wanted us to and, in the end, we didn't feel good. Remember, monitor how you feel, as this is a key indicator of whether you are in alignment. Are your predominant thoughts positive or negative about the situation and how does it make you feel?

We need to detach from what others think of us. When we are worried about someone else's opinion about what we have said or done, we need to ask ourselves why? We need to go inside and seek our own truth. We know what we truly want and who we really are. We simply need to be willing to ask the right questions and then to be honest with ourselves when we seek the answers.

## Detaching from Outcomes

Most of us have dreams, desires and intentions for ourselves. Sometimes those dreams, desires and intentions get so strong that we get attached to how and when our desires manifest. We want things to happen right now, and we want things to unfold the way we think they should unfold.

What we need to do is detach from outcomes and, in particular, how and when they manifest. Sometimes we get so focused on what we want that we start to obsess and wonder why it isn't happening. Ask the question: How does this make me feel? It usually does not make you feel good. In fact, it often produces negative thoughts and questions like, Why hasn't it happened yet? Why can't I find the person of my dreams, or that next great career opportunity? What's wrong with me?

Detachment is about having dreams and desires and then letting them go into the universe, with no attachment. When we are so focused on how and when something manifests, we often have blinders on our eyes, like the horse that is encouraged to only look straight ahead. When you do this, you miss all of the amazing things around you. When you detach and let go of your desires and dreams, you can relax and focus on your own truth. You can live in the present and have gratitude for what you do have in your life. This builds forward motion.

This does not mean that you stop doing the things that will assist you in creating those desires and dreams; you simply don't attach a specific method or timeline to the results. You move forward, doing the things that are in alignment with your desires, but you are not emotionally attached to how and when they arrive. You let go and let be. You remain open to all possibilities. You are much more likely to see opportunity when you are not attached and intensely focused on only one outcome.

Remember, your primary goal is to have the right thoughts, feelings and emotions about your desires so that you will take the right actions to produce the best outcomes. If you are attached, you will run the risk of overriding the good feeling thoughts you need to manifest your intentions or desires with impatience and frustration. This is because when you are detached, but not disengaged, you will not have negative thoughts when things don't manifest exactly as you thought they should. For example, if you are looking for a new job and going on interviews, you can become very attached emotionally to the outcomes and results of every job interview. If you go to an interview and then spend the next six days waiting for that phone call, thinking about it every day and obsessing about whether this is the one or not, you create potentially negative feelings when the job does not come your way. However, when you detach and simply go to the interview knowing that if it is meant to be, you will be made a great offer, you are able to move forward much more positively. If the job offer does not come, you are able to simply say, "Next time" or "This was obviously not the right one." You move quickly and effortlessly through the news with little or no disappointment. The opposite is attachment where you can begin to think all kinds of negative thoughts like, *What's wrong with me, why can't I find that great job? Why didn't they want me?* How do these thoughts serve you? They don't! When you are leading-self and spiritually aligned you interview better and bring the real you to the meeting.

Organizational leaders can learn a lot from detachment. In business we are great at creating a long list of goals and initiatives. We get heavily focused and often rigid in our approach to accomplishing objectives. We are so attached to outcomes that we often miss opportunities because we are going down one road and one road only. We build a plan for the next year and we stick to that plan, without staying open to changes or possibilities.

Organizations that truly and intrinsically know who they are, with a clear compelling purpose, will have intentions and desires for outcomes and will lay out a plan. However, they will detach, not disengage, from rigid roadmaps. They will stay open to possibilities and they will be on the lookout for new and exciting ways of accomplishing goals. Detachment is the ability of an organization to remain in alignment with their compelling purpose, have intentions and desires for outcomes, but stay open to how and when they manifest. This leads to innovation, creativity and open-mindedness as to how goals are accomplished. It creates an organizational environment where everyone aligns to the compelling purpose with vigor and enthusiasm, while staying flexible to the process as to how to accomplish goals. This is imperative in today's fast paced and ever-changing business environment. Remember it does not mean we don't have plans and roadmaps, it simply means we don't get attached to one way and one way only to accomplish desired outcomes. We move forward working toward our objectives, but are open, detached and on the lookout for new ways and opportunities to get where we want to go.

I realize that this may seem way too unstructured and willy-nilly for an organization to be effective; however, it is important to note that we still need to move in a forward direction with the right thoughts, feelings, behaviors and actions, which we already know will produce the right outcomes.

The most successful organizations and leaders are adaptable and flexible in their approach to creating success. This also creates an environment where leaders and employees can utilize creativity and be on the lookout for opportunity at any time, because the organization has created a context that encourages and rewards this type of thinking. This is Spiritually Aligned Leadership that has permeated throughout the organization.

# CHAPTER NINE

# CREATING THE LIFE AND WORK YOU WERE DESTINED TO HAVE

I have attempted to create a roadmap that parents, leaders and every individual can follow that will assist them in going inside, becoming honest about who they are, and what they want. It's a journey to uncover one's internal truth. It is important however that I make it very clear that this work is NOT about suddenly changing your life, quitting your job or leaving your marriage. In fact is the exact opposite. It is about *Taking No Action*.

We live in a world that has trained us to think in terms of doing, meeting objectives, creating plans and taking action. Spiritually Aligned Leadership is about a journey of self-discovery, a willingness to be honest with oneself and the courage to explore and challenge our old ways of thinking. It is anything but easy, but in some ways it is very easy, as it requires no actual action. There are no *decisions to be made*.

As an individual begins to ask themselves the hard questions about life, work and leadership, they become the Observer. They monitor what they are thinking about and how it makes them feel.

If they determine that their thoughts do not serve them well, they make a simple decision to change what they think about. They also begin to monitor how they feel.

Now this sounds easier than it is. Most individuals need some daily practices that will assist them in changing what they think about. Those daily practices usually start with writing out some simple affirmations and placing them strategically around the house. Remember to start with something simple. If your dominant negative thought is about your weight and health then you need to write out affirmations about how great you are going to feel when you are more fit, how attractive you are and how you accept yourself for exactly who you are. It might mean hanging some inspiring pictures in high traffic areas. You have to replace the unwanted negative thoughts about yourself and your situation if you are to begin to change what you think about.

If your negative thoughts are about your employment and career, imagine yourself doing something different, something you really love. Write affirmations and visualize being happy at work. It is definitely not about quitting your job—it begins with changing what you think about.

Next, you might get out a journal and begin a daily practice of journaling about what it will be like when you create that new situation or change. You will include statements of gratitude and appreciation for all that you have. You will begin to write about all the great things you currently have in your life and what you are thankful for. Even that job, that you dislike so much, has some good attributes. You are beautiful and you know you are a good person, so start writing about it every day. Ten minutes each morning or evening is a great time to journal.

You will begin to catch yourself when you have negative thoughts, feelings or behavior and you will be grateful for your increased awareness of this. You are the Observer of YOU. You might need to detach or accept things as they are. You need to consider your judgments of a situation or person and decide that this is not who you want to be. Remember the Tools of Intention are simple tools that allow us to evaluate when we might be derailing and why. Remember that how you *feel* is a key indicator of whether you are in alignment or not, so if you don't feel good ask yourself, Why? You may also want to ask yourself: Was I trying to climb someone else's tree? Was I trying to put my beliefs, values and opinions onto another person? Was I trying to lead someone else when what I would prefer to do is lead myself? It might require that you detach and let go. Live and let live!

You should not berate yourself for being negative or for judging another person's choices, but you will acknowledge it. Ask yourself the question: Is this who I want to be? How do these judgments serve me? Then you can make a different choice. You will let it go quickly and then journal about how you moved through easily and returned to equilibrium, balance and the intentional YOU. This is something you should be very proud of.

Note that it is truly a practice that requires simple, subtle, tiny steps each day. There are no big changes and no major decisions made about life and work. However, some of these very simple changes in your thought process can make you feel very uneasy and totally off balance. You have begun to challenge everything you have known about our old energy society, relationship with your employer, work colleagues and family. There is a strange contradiction that most people experience right away. On the one hand you begin to feel a sense of relief and that you are on the right path, but on the other hand you feel uneasy, awkward and that you might be shifting away from societal norms. This can be scary. It's okay—this is so normal. It is critical that you are easy with these shifts; that you don't make any demands of yourself or expect any kind of perfection. Monitor the Ego and the conversations with your Roommate. Be easy with yourself.

Your daily practice and observation of your thoughts will eventually lead to finding more small activities that support your new choices. Those activities might include reading something each day that aligns with your new beliefs or which challenges your thinking on spirituality and wellness. As you expand your thinking you might then want to consider adding in a daily practice of meditation, seeking reflection and a time and place for going inside, quieting the mind and turning to your heart-center for guidance. You want to connect to your true self. Remember you have made no life decisions or any drastic moves; you simply made a choice to learn about you and to become self-centered. How fabulous!

As you create your own Tree of Abundance you might experience some other changes within yourself. You may slowly, without any fanfare or acknowledgement, change your diet, start walking in nature, reduce or even eliminate the need for alcohol. You may take up yoga or another form of physical activity. You may discover that some of your relationships with friends might start to change. Some friends might be curious about your changes and want to inquire while others will sense a need to step back. I need to add something here that can be uncomfortable for some, but needs to be clearly stated. Some of your family and friends will not like the changes. Some will be afraid that you will leave them behind as you grow and evolve. Some might criticize your choices because they think you are being selfish; that you should consider others' feelings first and that you should conform. This is old energy and this is what we have been doing as a species for over 300 years. It doesn't work, so be aware of this and be okay with it. Let people know that you are just becoming who you truly want to be and that you completely accept them for who they are. You do not judge them for their choices and you do not believe your choices are better; you simply are changing. Detach and accept things as they are. Sometimes those that are the most upset are those that like the old you. They like the person that would go for coffee or a glass of wine and talk about others in a negative way. They like the old judgmental, conforming you. Unfortunately conflict or simple unrest can emerge because your friends or family members maybe feel forced to look at themselves as they look at you. You begin to put out a new, different and lighter energy and as a result others who interact with you may begin to feel uneasy and sense that maybe they should shift. Or that perhaps they are not in alignment. It is critical at this stage that you continue creating your own Tree of Abundance and that you do not try to influence others to come on your journey. Some will be very curious and will want more, others will retreat and move on. Some will not be comfortable being around you any more because your choices are so very different. What you had in common in the past no longer unites you. I am still friends with most of the people I was friends with prior to my major shift; however, I don't see them as much as I did in the past. I love them unconditionally for who they are; that will never change. The cool part is, new people come into your life who are exploring the same things you are and who are seeking their unique truth. New conversations emerge and a gentle shift begins to happen.

I don't believe that any of this is easy and yet the rewards are unbelievable. You begin to feel like the co-creator of your life again. You are never a victim, only a creator of your own path, the nurturer of your own tree. You have begun to have very clear images in your mind of who you are and where you want to go next. You have created confidence and an *inner knowing*. Herein lies the fabulous reward; at this stage of your journey, which could be years, months, weeks or in my case decades. There are no decisions that need to be made, there is simply a *knowing*.

What do I mean by this? You find yourself slowly undergoing changes, moving in a direction that aligns with your new desires and intentions. You may begin to initiate something new or purge something old, but not because you have made a typical *big decision*. It comes from a deep knowing in the heart-center, not from a left-brain cerebral perspective. You simply know from deep inside what needs to be done and you are fully comfortable. You might know that it is time to change your career, or relationship or re-align your business activities. You might decide you need to move or go traveling. None of this will have happened overnight and none of it will be on a whim or from a *laissez-faire* perspective. You are NOT on auto-pilot reacting to life. You will find yourself slowly, with no real fanfare at all, moving in a new direction with patience, focus and clear intent. This does not mean you will have no fear and that you will be perfect at all this *new stuff*, but what it does mean is that even though you still have some fear, and those periodic negative conversations with your Ego, you will respond effectively and clearly, knowing that you are slowly and strategically moving in the right direction and it will come from a very different place. It will come from a place deep inside your heart-center. It will simply feel right.

Although you will have a clear image of where you want to end up, or the change you want to see, you will be detached and open to allowing the universe to co-create with you. Which means that you are open to seeing where it takes you and you are not attached to it unfolding in a specific and structured way. This is truly where the fun is. You are comfortable with ambiguity. You are on the path. Your tree is clearly planted, growing and evolving and there is a knowing that a change is coming, but you are not rigid in how the change occurs; you do not have a rigid plan. You allow the sun and wind to assist in guiding the way; when and how your tree takes shape. This is where the scary excitement begins. I do mean scary excitement, because that is exactly what it feels like. You are nervous and yet so excited knowing that you are on the right path and when asked if you are sure about the direction you are going, you simply and clearly respond, "I wouldn't change a thing."

As you move toward your new intention, don't be surprised if you have some fear, especially if you are letting go of things that you have held onto for some time. You simply need to ask yourself: Do I know for sure this is what I want? Am I in alignment with what I know to be true for me? If the answers are, *Yes* then be brave and simply put one foot in front of the other. This is when amazing things will begin to happen. Each one of us is intended to seek our joy and passion and to find amazing ways to contribute to our communities, families and workplaces. As you move toward your truth, opportunities will present themselves. Often these opportunities are more fabulous than you could have ever imagined. You are worth amazing abundance and you know it. You love yourself fully and it feels great.

# PART III

# THE **MANY ROLES** OF SPIRITUALLY ALIGNED LEADERSHIP

# CHAPTER TEN

# THE MOST IMPORTANT ROLE, BEING A PARENT

What a huge topic this is; and one that is very sensitive for all of us. We can discuss almost anything with others, but the way we choose to raise our children is usually off limits. It is considered a sacred right, one of the most personal things we will ever do and we take it very seriously. In my opinion, we take it way too seriously, which can get us into trouble. Regardless of how sensitive this subject matter is, I want to share a viewpoint that might seem radical, but one that I believe is worth serious consideration.

When we teach our Creating Positive Energy—Parenting classes we often begin by asking each participant what they hope to get out of the class. Then we let them know that one of the most important things they can do is detach from their children. We state, "The sooner you learn to detach from your children, the healthier your relationships will be." The reactions we get from our workshop participants are priceless. It is in that moment that the participant thinks, *What did I just sign up for? Do I stay and listen to this crazy person or do I walk right out that door?* Another question I love to ask is, "How did you like it when you were fourteen or fifteen years old and your parents continually told you what you could and could not do?" Most of our attendees respond by saying, "I hated it." I then ask, "So why, when we become parents do we do exactly the same thing to our children?" The definition of detachment is important when considering both of these questions and we will continue to deepen our understanding of it.

In this chapter, we consider children and parenting from a variety of perspectives. I will begin by discussing the gifts and talents I have seen within children as young as two and three years old and how we need to offer our children opportunities to truly tap into these gifts as early as possible. We will compare and contrast parenting styles—the traditional hands on, fear-based, old energy style versus parenting with higher vibrational energy and Spiritual Alignment. In Chapter One we discussed the importance of seeking the truth about our story. Children will ultimately have their own story. We will explore the importance of your child's story and the value, as a parent, in seeking the truth about that story. I will also touch on our education system, which is screaming for full reform, but is so buried in dogma, politics and bureaucracy that they just can't seem to make the shift. Lastly, we look at the factors of unconditional love and why it is critical that we detach from our children so that all parties can experience unconditional love.

If you are a baby boomer or even a person over the age of forty with young adult children, you may have discovered that your children are incredibly smart. My experience is they are brighter and certainly more intuitive than I was at the same age. At twenty-five they may be reading books or researching topics online you didn't even consider reading until you were well into your 40s. They are asking the hard questions about life. They are making tough decisions and taking a stand against the dogma and protocol of a typical life in the mainstream, corporate world. They talk about joy, passion, seeking balance and wanting to truly be connected to what they do. They do not want to simply fit in; they want to thrive, seek their joy and love what they do.

Many of the young adults today jump from job to job seeking an employer who actually knows what their compelling purpose is, why they are in business, and how the average front line employee fits into that purpose. Leaders (organizations) with old energy simply believe that they are working with a generation that is flippant and not focused. They prefer to believe there is something wrong with today's younger employee. It certainly couldn't have anything to do with their organization, how it is run or how people are treated. Some organizations truly believe that they will be able to continue to operate from this old energy perspective. However the young people of today are changing this quickly as they will not settle for working in a valueless and out of alignment organization. Our newest employees will change the business world forever.

## Special Gifts from Our Special Little Ones

As mentioned in Chapter Five, children are not born as blank slates; rather they are born with incredible gifts and talents, passions and personalities. Our role as a parent is to assist our children in discovering those gifts and talents, and more importantly encouraging our children to be true to themselves, to become Spiritually Aligned Leaders. This means that children must be given the opportunity to explore their interests and find their passions. When do they feel most happy? What brings them the most joy?

If we believe that people are born naturally good, seeking to have a positive impact on themselves and the world around them, then we need to recognize that our children are no different. If we approach parenting from this perspective, we'll see our young children as naturally good, with dreams and passions and a desire to seek their greatest joy. We also are more likely to see how smart, intuitive and sensitive to energy they are. However, if we believe that our parenting role is to teach them to be good, we bring immediate judgments of good and bad and they begin to sense this.

I love to ask the interesting and intriguing questions, like: Is it possible that our children are born already feeling the goodness of the world and already connected to their inner truth, but through our biases, judgments and well-meaning parenting we fill them with a list of right and wrong, good and bad?

Parents often believe that their role is to influence and direct their children and to ensure that their children fit in with what is expected within a normal society. We sometimes believe that *fitting in* creates happiness. We want them to be successful, and our definition of success informs our guidance. As a result, we begin to influence our children right from the beginning.

We need to challenge our thinking about parenting because our children might just have the right answers for themselves—if given a chance to consider their options and to explore who they are. Children are no different than adults. They need to be encouraged to go inside and seek their truth, to practice Spiritually Aligned Leadership, to monitor how they feel and to be able to explore what those feelings mean.

My strong curiosity about young children today has given me the opportunity to talk to a lot of parents and meet a lot of children. I am seeing some of the most amazing and odd gifts. One little boy has been meditating since before his mother can remember. He calls it going to peace. He seems to be able to detach and leave the outside world behind whenever he needs to. He goes inside and seeks his own truth and is able to talk about it with his mom. She had never meditated before, nor had her husband, but their young son does this naturally and comfortably. Another little girl is attracted to bugs and in particular to butterflies. This might not seem like something special, but imagine walking outside on a beautiful summer day and having every butterfly in the neighborhood come for a visit, land on your head, arms and legs just to say, *hi*. One of the other things that I have noticed, and many parents have spoken to me about, is the early age at which some children begin to speak and form sentences. In one case an eighteen month old is speaking full sentences as if he were born fluent in English. I am not sure this is an isolated example.

We've also had the opportunity to work with parents of children who have been diagnosed with ADHD. Many of these parents are scared and frustrated, as the system does not support the needs of these children. The answer they receive, in most cases, is that their child needs to be drugged to fit into society, to make it easier to learn. One of the fastest growing pharmaceutical markets is that of medication for our children. I believe there is something deeply wrong with this. In one case, a parent described their twelve year old hiding his medication all over the house. Their son would put his pills in the freezer, under the couch and hide them in the sheets of his bed. When she asked him why he was so reluctant to take his medication, he simply responded by saying, "When I'm on those pills no one asks me how I am."

Our experience, with these young people, is that they are smart beyond our understanding. They see the world through a completely different lens and our lack of understanding and inability to recognize the child's unique talents and gifts leaves parents frustrated and scared. These parents describe a *sense of knowing* that their child is special, and incredibly smart. Deep down they know their child has gifts that have not been tapped into. As these mothers and fathers become more Spiritually Aligned and begin to detach from expected outcomes, they are able to look for the special abilities within their child. They see their child as a unique and gifted individual. When we speak with these parents we simply ask questions: Does your son/daughter have any special gifts or talents? When do you notice them focusing? Do you think your son/daughter is smart? The answers are almost always the same, "absolutely, so smart, just really different."

What does this tell me? It tells me that we are not looking for the right things; we are not accessing their gifts and talents because we have a predetermined system that does not have the time or resources to allow this type of exploration. However, this is exactly what the child needs—time and space to explore their gifts and talents and to be asked directly and authentically what jazzes or interests them. With this information we could expose them to as many things as possible that actually have meaning to them.

Some parents have simply decided to accept that it is best for their child to coast through the education system while exploring their true interests at home and in the community. They give the child permission to not take any of it too seriously and to simply get by, all the while they are finding opportunities for their children to explore their true greatness and joy on their own.

A positive environment is critical to creating a healthy space for our children to grow and explore the world. This environment can only be created through the development of the parents' Spiritual

Alignment; the process of *leading-self*. As the parents focus on their work to uncover their truth and become Spiritually Aligned, they monitor the conversations with their Roommate and begin to tell a different story; a positive and uplifting story about the gifts, intellect and abilities of their child. As the parents lead themselves, they begin to see the situation quite differently. Many have shared stories with us about being able to finally see the special gifts that their children have and they can now encourage the development of those gifts. They look at their child completely differently and they begin to get different results.

## Old Energy Parenting vs. Higher Vibrational (Positive) Energy

By the time the average child is eighteen months to two years old, most parents have begun to say *no* a lot. "Don't do this." "Don't touch that." "Don't say this." "Don't say that." We quickly fill our children's world with a lot of negativity. We don't do this intentionally and we don't even see it in these terms. We believe we are keeping them safe, directing them to be accepted in society, creating respectful language; the list goes on and on.

If we are really honest with ourselves, we will admit that a lot of our parenting is based on lack and fear, not on abundance, trust and positive energy. I know this sounds harsh, but much of our old parenting energy is fundamentally based on society's expectations, which includes specific expectations for our children. We take the parenting role extremely seriously and often underneath it is fear of failure as a parent. The ability for children to sense energy allows them to pick up on this at a very young age.

If we believe that our children are smart and that they are inherently good at heart then why not change our approach? Ask your children questions so that they can consider the right answers for themselves. I know this may seem a bit weird at first, to actually believe that children as young as two or three years old would have the right answer for themselves, but they do. Most parents just aren't prepared to take the time to ask the child the important series of questions to allow them to explore the answers. It is often perceived as easier to provide the answer to the child, and to build expectations that there is a right way and wrong way to handle every situation. When we slow down and ask a series of questions, the child can explore how they feel about a situation and inevitably make great choices.

It is important that the parent monitor their own thoughts and beliefs about their child if they are to successfully assist their children in seeking the answers for themselves. Every time a parent allows a child to seek their own truth and alignment, they are assisting them in learning to become a Spiritually Aligned Leader themselves, to trust their inner voice or internal guidance system. We send the child a clear message; "I trust you and your decision-making. I believe your feelings are important and that you need to ask yourself the hard questions." We can begin to expose our children to the Tools of Intention from a very early age. Encouraging them to be truly honest with themselves first and foremost is critical.

Young children truly want to make their parents happy. They are usually seeking approval and love and tune into the parents' energy to see if they are pleasing them or not. Spiritually Aligned parents make it very clear to the child that they should seek their own joy and happiness. Parents need to be very careful with this, as often our children will appear to be doing what they want, but in fact are simply trying to please us. Children often behave according to what they believe the parents want to see or hear. Our young children are incredibly sensitive to energy within the household so they can easily sense what will make the parent happy.

We need to expose our children to the concept of *going within* to seek their personal truth, or what feels good to them and be open to their truth, even if that truth does not align with mainstream ideologies. A Spiritually Aligned parent will ask the child how it makes them feel and will help the child understand the significance and correlation between how they feel and the results they get. They let the child know at every opportunity to trust their heart-center and to align themselves with great feeling thoughts. They let the child know that they have faith in their ability to make great decisions based on how it makes them feel. They allow the child to use this skill as a key indicator as to whether a decision is a good one or a bad one. And of course the parent is a fabulous role model, seeking their own truth and alignment, and monitoring what they think about and how they feel.

One single parent recently told us a story about applying the Tools of Intention for herself as she interacted with her four year old son and how she has created a completely different relationship with him. In her words, "I finally see my son as a completely separate person detached from me." One of the many examples she has shared with us is their bedtime routine. Bedtime used to be a horrible experience, rife with negative energy. Her son would do everything to prolong staying up. He wouldn't listen when asked to brush his teeth and eventually both of them would end up angry and frustrated. Words would be exchanged that were not in alignment. Now, if things get out of alignment, she simply says to her son, "Mom really loves you and does not want to be angry with you or to argue with you, so I am going to go into the kitchen and make a nice cup of tea. I think it would be better if we simply took a minute to be on our own." She refuses to fight or argue with her son about bedtime routines or timing and the energy has shifted. Most evenings her son gets himself ready for bed, focusing on timing that works for him and makes sure to have a quiet story time with mom before falling asleep. His mother does not make threats or ultimatums. She simply does what she needs to do to stay balanced, detached and in alignment. As she does that and shares her strategy with her son, he begins to understand. She sets a clear example of Spiritually Aligned Leadership.

This may seem like a simple example, but when applied to other issues it works extremely well. For example, we teach our children from a very young age that they have to share everything and to ensure that everyone gets a turn. This is absolutely counter-intuitive and makes no sense. We teach our children not to be selfish and to consider the needs of others first and then we wonder why they don't know themselves, don't know what they want or what makes them happy. We encourage children to put the needs of others before their own needs, which sends a clear message; others' feelings and needs are to be valued more importantly than their own. This includes the feelings and needs of the parents. We tell our children not to be selfish, but at the same time we encourage them to do what we want them to do. No wonder many of our children are confused. As we attempt to teach them to be good citizens, good team members, good friends and a good little girl or boy, the message is, *fit in by making others happy.*

Spiritually Aligned Leaders believe that people, including children, should be self-centered and that they can be self-centered without being selfish. If you are not seeking your joy, no one else will seek it for you. It simply will not get done. Your children are no different. The only person that can seek your child's joy is your child. Your job is to encourage them to do this at every stage of their life; to go inside and seek the answers, to be true to themselves and to not be held back by fear. Their job is not to make you happy!

Remember that if you believe that all people are born good at heart and that children are good-natured then you must have confidence that when you encourage them to go inside and seek their truth and joy, that their truth and joy will include consideration of others. When they make a decision to please someone else, they will do it with free will and joy, not because of societal expectations, or worse, guilt.

What we put out is what we will get back. The world mirrors back at us. So if you want your children to talk to you about their life you must first share your life with them. Old parent energy believed that you should not share your problems or challenges with your children. We often didn't talk to our children about work or money, joys or sorrows. Don't believe that they are not capable of understanding and caring about your dreams and desires. When we are open and candid with our young children, allowing them to see us as vulnerable human beings, with goals, joys, challenges and obstacles, they will share their hopes, dreams and desires with us.

The goal is to ensure that your children do not put you on a pedestal. Remember, *no one in front or behind.* This includes the parent-child relationship. When your children believe that they are just as important as you are and that their dreams, desires and opinions on issues are just as valid, they cannot lose themselves. They will become confident and Spiritually Aligned adults. They will learn to value and appreciate their inner voice and to monitor how they feel. Our job is to create a context that enables this.

**Education**

Before sharing my views on the present state of our educational system in North America, I want to state that I am aware my views are strong and controversial. This does not mean that I do not appreciate the complexity of this system and the incredible work teachers and administrators contribute to trying to provide great education. I simply believe it is an old energy system that needs reform.

The school system, in its attempt to make school a safe and meaningful place, has unintentionally undervalued the Tools of Intention and the ability of students to make great decisions. There is a rule for everything because the school system is worried about losing control. There may be a belief that if they allowed the children to direct themselves and make decisions on their own there would be anarchy; everyone out for themselves. If we go inside and ask ourselves, do we really believe this is true, the answer is *no*. For those who believe this is true, and that there would be chaos, your belief is based on lack, fear and uncertainty.

Unfortunately our school system is in deep crisis and is struggling to find reform that will work. We continue to teach to a strict curriculum and not to the individual child. How could we ever believe that one set of standards would work for every child? I know it can be overwhelming to believe that we could build a reformed school system that would honor the unique gifts and talents of each child; a system that would engage the child at a young age, based on what they want to learn, but this is in fact what we need to do. We need to seek creative ways to assist our children in learning what they are truly interested in; giving them choices that would allow them to experience their natural abilities. Instead, we worry about whether they will learn to read at the precise moment they should be reading.

Recently, I worked with a concerned mother who had received a call from the school about her son. He was not progressing with his handwriting at the rate the school felt he should be. I do not believe that I have the answers for anyone else, but I do believe I can ask good questions. I simply asked the mother if she had asked her son how he felt about handwriting. She immediately answered, "Yes, I did ask him and he said he didn't care about handwriting, that it was an old art that was great for some people, but that he had no interest." I then asked her how she felt about it. She agreed that if he was not interested she saw no reason why he should learn this skill. Her primary concern was how to have a conversation with the school and the teacher about their discovery. The son simply didn't want to learn to do handwriting. Was this so horrible? In the education system in particular, we often work to the system and not to the child. The more important question was, what was her son truly interested in and was he being given an opportunity to explore his true interests.

Children disengage from school because they are bored, bored, bored. We are not teaching them things that are of real interest to them. We believe that they need to learn to read and write on a predetermined time frame, when in fact some children are brilliant in other areas, but have absolutely no interest in reading. They won't pick up reading until they find something they are truly interested in reading about. Then it will come to them effortlessly. Because schools are teaching to a predetermined schedule, they don't consider the needs of the individual child and don't ask them what they want to learn about. They don't provide a child any electives or voice in their own learning until Grade Six or Seven, when a child is usually eleven or twelve years of age. Do we believe that children do not have a preference until this age or do we simply think that they have to learn things on a predetermined schedule? Or maybe we believe that the school system (teachers/administrators/parents) knows best. We absolutely do not have a system that honors the individual learner. It serves the system itself, but not those it was originally designed to educate.

I do believe that the system was useful and met an important need in the past, but the rapid changes taking place on our planet today require a brand new approach and a mechanism to allow parents and teachers to easily engage with children in a way that encourages the child to seek their own interests, skills, gifts and natural abilities. If we provide an environment that allows the child to excel in their own way, on their own time frame, we might be able to change the engagement level within the education system. If we let our children lead the way in redesigning the education system, we might end up with a product that is efficient, effective and one that honors the gifts of all children. We simply need to imagine the future possibilities where children can attend a school system that makes them the focus of the learning, where they have choices right from the beginning and a system that allows them to learn when and how they need to learn.

Of course we would have to ultimately believe that children are not born as blank slates and that they do have interests, gifts and natural abilities right from the beginning. We would have to be Spiritually Aligned Leaders ourselves to know and trust that when children are allowed to seek their own truth they will not go wrong. If the individual makes a poor decision that has a negative impact, they consider what they were thinking about at the time, whether Ego was involved, and what they might do differently to improve the situation. If we have set a great example of Spiritually Aligned Leadership, they will know to go inside and seek the truth. As parents, our role is to trust in this and to encourage our children to trust themselves; to love themselves and to know that they are here to seek their greatest good and highest joy by nurturing their true interests and uniqueness. We understand that each child has his own Tree of Abundance and that they are supposed to climb their own tree, have their own journey. Many parents spend significant amounts of time climbing their sons' and daughters' trees and then wondering why they are not getting the results they want.

## What is Your Child's Story?

I believe in the power of stories and the importance of sharing our stories. All three of my sons tell their stories as a way of assisting others in learning that our stories do not have to define us forever. In Chapter Five, Becoming the Observer, I briefly wrote about our youngest son's journey through the school system and his inability to read and write at the pace in which the system wanted him to.

Bob and I made one bad decision after another trying to get Mike to fit within a system that just didn't work for him. However, the entire time, we knew how smart and talented he was. He had a very special gift with verbal communication and articulation of thoughts. He connected to people in a way that most adults practice for years before becoming competent.

Our poor decisions and a system that didn't work for Mike created a series of events that had Mike move from one school to the next as we tried to find the right learning environment. Our intentions were good and of course we only wanted the best for him, but what did we actually do? What was the message we sent Mike on a regular basis? The message was, *Mike you are not smart enough. Mike you need extra help to get caught up. Mike you need to learn to read this year.* Regardless of how many times we told Mike we loved him and how smart we thought he was, our actions were about what he lacked and how we needed him to catch up with the other kids. Mike interpreted this as, *I am stupid, and I am not smart enough. Why am I so different?* If you ask Mike now he can clearly articulate how bored he was and how he could not understand why he had to learn some of the useless things that he was being taught.

Mike was extremely curious about quantum physics even though he did not know what quantum physics was. He naturally understood sacred geometry, although he struggled with basic math. He was incredibly futuristic and had a natural ability to think in terms of possibilities.

I've reflected on how different the outcome would have been if my husband and I had been Spiritually Aligned Leaders. What if we had been able to observe our thoughts and feelings and we had listened to our inner voice? We would have made very different choices and we would have focused on Mike's gifts and not worried about what the school system said. The messages Mike received from us would have been very different, and Mike would have had very different thoughts and feelings. I suspect he would have recognized his exceptional gifts earlier in life. I believe he would have flourished instead of losing so many years of his life feeling he was stupid and less than others.

Every child has a story, just like every adult has a story. People who are parents of adult children and who are interested in pursuing Spiritually Aligned Leadership often benefit by having candid conversations with their children about their experiences growing up. They ask for honest and real feedback and go into the discussion as an exploration only, with no agenda and no desire to share their perspective with the child—only to listen and learn. The parent approaches the conversation from the perspective of simply, *I want to know what it was like from the child's vantage point with no opinions or views or emotions around this experience.* They approach the discussion with acceptance, detachment and a willingness to learn. There is no right or wrong, just simply a perspective of *it is what it is.*

As a parent, it is important to understand that your intention is not what matters, it is the message that the child receives that matters. When teaching a recent Creating Positive Energy workshop, a parent shared a story about her fifteen year old son who, from her perspective, was gifted in math and science. She believed that he could do extremely well if he pursued a Science degree once he finished high school. She appeared to be very attached to this idea. She indicated that her son, however, was not meeting his potential and that he would often bring home exam marks that were far below what he was capable of. I asked her what she would say to him on these occasions. She replied, "I simply let him know how smart I think he is and that he is not meeting his potential and he could easily get an 'A' instead of the 'C'." She stated that she only wanted the best for him—which of course is true. But herein lies the problem—what is the message her son received? It may not have been her intention to tell her son that he had let her down, that he was not good enough, that he could do better, but this was what her son heard. I simply said, "Don't you think, if he wanted to get an 'A' on the science exam he would get an 'A' on the science exam?"

We make these things about us, not about our child. We continually try to climb our children's Tree of Abundance instead of teaching them how to access it themselves. We internalize these things because we are attached to results that we believe are the right results. We often have a predetermined set of ideals, values or outcomes that we think our children should subscribe to. In truth, we want things for our children that they may not want for themselves. When we don't seek to understand what they want and allow them to explore their own gifts and talents and, more importantly, where their joy and love comes from, we undervalue their uniqueness and their own desires. We make parenting about us and not about the child.

As parents we must monitor and observe what we think about and ask ourselves the really hard questions. Am I making this about me? Has my child really made the decisions that are important to them without my heavy intentional influence? There is nothing easy about this, but the rewards are amazing. Spiritually Aligned Leadership creates relationships based on unconditional love and appreciation for uniqueness.

Many of us believe we have experienced Spiritually Aligned relationships. However I would challenge this. Most of us have never actually internalized the feelings of either being unconditionally loved or giving unconditional love. Unconditional love is that absolute knowing that your love flows freely and effortlessly regardless of the choices your children make. This is the toughest concept to understand and even tougher to apply. As parents we believe we love our children unconditionally, even when they do something that we disagree with. However, if you have any attachments resulting in negative thoughts or judgments regarding their choices, you cannot have or give unconditional love. It is when you are able to release all judgments about another person's journey that you find unconditional love. When you are able to accept that each person, including your children, have their own Tree of Abundance and are on their own journey, you are able to experience unconditional love. You intentionally detach and do not allow yourself to climb the tree of another person. You stand on the sidelines with acceptance and non-judgment as your fundamental root system.

The challenge arises when we internalize and make their choices about us. This is when we get into trouble. If we can detach, and accept things the way they are, then we can create unconditional love. It requires that we acknowledge, as the parent, we would not make that same choice for ourselves. The parent stays on his or her own tree, focused on *leading-self* with no judgment of the other.

This does not mean that the important conversations do not take place. The parent and child should explore issues together by asking great questions. It simply means that if the parent wants to truly experience unconditional love, they have to remain climbing their own tree while having no negative judgments about the direction their child's tree is growing. These are the toughest concepts for parents to understand. We have been so conditioned to lead, direct and facilitate every area of our child's life that this just seems so odd. However, if you go inside and truly ask yourself, and you really listen, you will come to the conclusion that this is how it is meant to be. Sometimes the easiest way to think about this is to consider how you felt as a child growing up.

Parents believe that parenting is the toughest job. Through our thoughts and feelings as parents we create challenges. It is our attachment to certain outcomes that creates friction between parent and child and between child and society. I know that these concepts are not easy, however, once you begin to practice detachment you will be pleasantly surprised at the rewards that unfold in front of you. The relationship that manifests between child and parent can be extremely rewarding. At one moment the parent is the teacher having organic influence by simply being Spiritually Aligned and the next moment the child becomes the teacher or mentor as the parent listens with intensity and seeks to understand a new concept or perspective. Higher vibrational energy between parent and child creates a relationship that is so rewarding and expansive. This is the framework for unconditional love.

# CHAPTER ELEVEN

# YOUR SIGNIFICANT OTHER

Many of us have a very strange way of looking at our intimate relationships. For some reason we believe that we must have lots of things in common, and that we must enjoy the same activities. Most of us look for someone with common values and common interests. What is fascinating—and we often don't realize in the beginning of a relationship—is that over time individuals change significantly, and it is very rare that two people will continue to have the same interests, or even the same values.

I would suggest that one of the major issues we have within our intimate relationships is that we lose our unique self. We become so entangled with the other person that sometimes we wonder, *Where am I?* We have discussed throughout the book the need to go inside and seek the answers for yourself and, most importantly, to seek *your* unique joy. This is the one thing we often do not do within our intimate relationships. Many of us still carry the old energy beliefs that to have a healthy relationship, we are supposed to do most things together and share the same interests.

Within a long-term relationship, people can become tired, feeling that years of compromise have worn them down. We then begin to look for relief. My question is, why compromise?

Now this question will strike some as being odd or insensitive. Am I implying that we should all just go out there and do whatever we want? Well, in fact I am suggesting just that. As Spiritually Aligned Leaders we follow our joy and seek our passion and within our long-term relationships, we encourage our partner to do the same. This encouragement comes from a place of unconditional love and a knowing that when a person seeks their joy and passions in life everything unfolds effortlessly.

In previous chapters we have talked about how a person can find relief practicing the Tools of Intention; letting go of the Ego, seeking happiness, joy and abundance instead of having to be right or to win. Life is not a race, and there are no winners and losers. There are, however, those who have taken the time and found the courage to seek their joy. They have faced their fears, and not looked back, even when it was really hard. This should also apply to our intimate relationships.

These relationships are often much harder to navigate through because there is so much entanglement. The individuals involved have often raised a family together and cohabitated for years and years. When one partner decides to change or alter the status quo, it can be very difficult on a long standing relationship. You may have begun to read self-help books or started a meditation practice. Maybe you are journaling every night as a way of getting your thoughts onto paper. You may have begun to ask the really hard questions about who you are and what you truly want, but if your partner is not the slightest bit interested in asking any of these questions, what do you do?

The answer is; you do *nothing!* It is not your job to push your partner in the same direction as yourself. Certainly, sharing with your partner what you are doing and what you are reading is great. Inviting your partner to the yoga or meditation classes is great also, but that's it. You invite only. The journey of Spiritually Aligned Leadership is a personal choice, and people must decide for themselves if they want to take that journey. You cannot insist or try to coerce your partner into coming on the ride. Remember this is not a bad thing; it is simply what they are comfortable with. Spiritually Aligned Leadership is an energy that is positive, creative and unique to each person. It must be a personal choice.

Herein lies the opportunity and the challenge. It can feel very chaotic within the relationship and very scary for the partner who prefers to remain with the old energy. They witness their partner letting go, becoming balanced, less intense. Maybe their partner starts to make some very unorthodox decisions about themselves, their career or money; it can be anything. They see situations and circumstances that once would have bothered their partner seem to melt away. They see their partner making very intentional and deliberate choices when dealing with the inevitable changes life brings. Parenting can become very challenging with each parent choosing a different path. All of this results in unrest and uneasiness, especially for the partner who is not interested in seeking this new energy. Maybe they see their partner of twenty or more years slowly changing how they interact with their adult children. During a time of life when most partners think things will be stable and finally settled (the kids are grown and making their own way in the world) they actually find themselves amidst turmoil and lots of unknown.

If you are making such changes in your life and your partner is not on the same path, you must be extremely sensitive to the situation and not attempt to change your partner. Be gentle, understanding and sensitive to their fears. As you are releasing fears and letting go, your partner might be having increased fears about the stability of your relationship. This is very normal. It is critical that you remember that you are only responsible for your journey and the choices you make. It is not your place or duty to try to convince someone to follow your new path. Do not climb your partner's tree.

It can also be very scary for the person who has decided to become a Spiritually Aligned Leader. As you follow your heart-center, you may begin to oppose the normal mainstream route. You may question many things within your relationship, which for years you simply accepted. All of this requires courage and the ability to face your fears. Remember that being honest with you is the key. You cannot be honest with anyone else if you are not honest with yourself first. You may be feeling that your relationship is changing too fast, or that you really want your partner to come along with you. You may begin to try to push the boulder up the hill and you may feel that you are going to have to detach. This part can be very scary.

You want to continue to move forward. You want to become balanced and to see the world as an abundant place full of opportunity, *not* full of challenges. You are grateful for everything and you do not see scarcity, only abundance. However, your partner may continue to see the old paradigms; the glass half empty and that life is a competition with not enough for everyone. Your partner may believe that there are the *haves* and the *have-nots*. You have begun to know that this simply isn't true, and you are creating amazing positive energy. Your relationship can begin to feel like a tumultuous unsettled and chaotic entanglement. This is very normal and an important stage in becoming a Spiritually Aligned Leader of yourself.

**Detangling**

Over time our intimate relationships become hugely enmeshed; where every important decision is made together, individuality is often lost and we work in tandem through all of life's challenges and situations. This creates a certain amount of emotional entanglement. We are connected in ways that we often don't even realize. We believe that we must be in alignment with each other and have the same values and want the same things. This belief is fundamentally flawed. We change over time and it is rare that two people will have the same needs, desires, values and interests. Often what makes our relationships great is how different we are. Over time however, we attempt to mold and shift our partner to see the world the same way we do. Spiritually Aligned Leaders don't have these expectations. If there is one common belief or value, it is that each person in the relationship needs to seek his or her own truth and alignment. We live in a world of free will, even if society tries to tell us otherwise, where each person is able to seek his or her own joy, abundance and positive energy.

If you have ever seen a picture of a rubber tree you know that it can grow around and around itself. I want you to imagine a rubber tree that has been growing into itself for thirty years, wrapped around and around, each root entangled in the next. This is how our primary relationships often feel. We build norms and routines for making decisions, interacting with family members and raising the children. Everything is tangled up with our partner. We don't even realize it until one of the partners decides to try something new. This is when we need to consider detangling.

Healthy relationships are not entangled. We cannot discover unconditional love when we are so enmeshed. In our old energy relationships, our love is often conditional and connected to agreeing on a common route. The way to envision healthy relationships based on unconditional love is to visualize two very separate roads with multiple bridges crossing back and forth. The idea is that you have your own separate and unique life and journey and you have numerous places to cross over and share. You could also imagine each person having their own Tree of Abundance with tree vines that once in a while swing over to your partner's branches for the opportunity to share in life's abundance. You share in the things that you want to share in and you can freely choose not to share in other areas of your partner's life. You love the other person for their differences and their willingness to be true to themselves; to seek their own path and to be willing to share it with you. You do not try to climb your partner's tree and they do not climb yours.

When I began on this journey many years ago, it was very scary for my partner. He spoke openly about his fear that I would leave him behind as I grew spiritually and learned to live a more balanced life. I was lucky that we had fabulous communication. Bob, who was approaching retirement, was worried that as I sought my own truth, it would not include him. This was never true for me; however, the process of detangling can be extremely slow and sometimes very painful. I was seeking my joy and passion and knew that I needed to let go of many things along the way so that I could make room for the new and amazing things that were going to come into my life. I had been exploring Spiritually Aligned Leadership for a couple of years and I had had the opportunity to try many of my theories within my human resource practice.

Bob and I were like many couples who had been married for thirty years, raised three children, had jobs and a house and still some debt. We had been through numerous life experiences together including almost losing my business, our son's significant difficulties and, like most couples, everything in between. We had our share of tough times, but here we were, about to go through another significant shift. We were both scared and unsure of what the future held. I was moving quickly along on my spiritual journey while Bob was more grounded in the here and the now of old energy. We could see that things were not the way they once used to be, and that scared us both.

As Bob prepared to retire from the only job he had ever known, my career was really beginning to take shape. I was truly following my passion. I was in love with my life and my work. He on the other hand had worked for thirty-seven years for the same organization and had always been the family's main provider. He was never really passionate about his work. It was a means to an end, as it is for many people, and it was definitely not Spiritually Aligned. He was tired. However, he also wanted to live on the west coast and has a unique relationship with nature, sailing and big trees. Living on the west coast was a true calling for him. It was the best place for him to be, so we made a decision that, after living together for twenty nine years, we were going to have two residences and we would live apart three weeks of every month. Our lives were about to become very rocky and very strange. We were going to learn to detangle in a *big* way.

For the past two years we have been slowly, and often painfully, watching the tree roots of the thirty year old rubber tree detangle. This may seem a little dramatic, but it is absolutely the truth and is the best way to describe it.

At one point my eldest son, Geoff, who is a gifted Medium, Spiritual Healer and Counseling Psychologist, became aware of how difficult this was for his dad and I. Although Bob and I had made a conscious and deliberate choice to live apart, and to begin to truly explore our unique joy and passion for life, it was not easy. Within the first year, I found myself at a crossroads. On the one hand I loved my new life and career and was living the dream of fulfillment and positive impact on others, and yet my long-term relationship with my life partner was at risk. It may seem weird to seek advice from your son, but in fact who better to consult than a person who truly loves both people? Geoff and I already had a highly evolved relationship, which was continuing to grow and expand at every opportunity. Talking to Geoff about what was going on just seemed like the most natural thing to do.

Like many young people, Geoff has some very special gifts due to his strong, intuitive energy. As a result, he has begun working as a medium where he is able to communicate with the Archangel Collective. After sharing my concerns and worries about my relationship with his dad, he had a meditation and was journaling when this message came to him. It was a message specifically for Bob and me. I received this email from Geoff early one Saturday morning while enjoying my morning coffee. I couldn't wait to forward it to Bob and to share what I had learned through this angel message.

Dearest Child,

You must first know that in these difficult times you are never alone. Our energy never leaves your side and our love is available to you at any moment. Our channel Tobin, who you call Geoff, felt that visualization may be of use to you while attempting to navigate your way through the haze and murkiness you now find yourself in. Your fears associated with your business, husband, and way of life can be compared to that of two individuals hiking through a forest and stumble upon two roads that will take them to the top of a very high mountain.

The first person feels that the road to the left is superior, it contains well lit pathways, open areas providing room for rest and safety, but the amount of time needed to get to the top is unknown. The first person is okay with the lengthy trip and prefers the path to the left.

The second person feels that the road to the right is by far the better choice because it has a clear and direct path to the top. The path is riskier, contains more room for error, but will take less time to reach the top therefore making it the more logical choice.

Herein lies the debate—which path makes more sense? They spend hours arguing, yelling, trying desperately to convince the other that their way of thinking is correct. Hours turn into days and finally, after all other resources have been depleted, they decide to seat themselves down on the ground and pray for the right answer to appear to both of them. While praying, they receive the exact same message: "Choose the path that fills you with joy, and trust in your Self." Both people open their eyes and understand what they must do. They hold hands and repeat the following words to each other.

The first person, looking in to the other's eyes says:

"I'm going to take the path on the left, I don't know how long it will take me to get to the top, but I promise that I will get there. When I am ready and have navigated the challenges that await me. My promise to you is that I will never stop trying to get to the top, if you promise to wait for me there, should you get there first."

The second person looking in to the other's eyes says:

"I'm going to take the path on the right, I don't know if I will survive the climb to the top, but I promise I will not proceed hastily. I will take my time and navigate the path as safely and carefully as I can. My promise to you is that I will never stop trying to get to the top, if you promise to wait for me there, should you get there first."

After both had spoken, they embraced and went along their journeys. The reason we share this story with you, dear one, is so that you understand that is okay to be on different paths to get to the top because, in the end, all roads will get you there. All that needs to exist is a promise that you will wait for them when you get there. And know that in your world, in physical form, no one really waits; we all get to where we need to be, at the exact same moment, when it is most perfect for us.

When you feel as though you have lost your way dear one, recite this prayer:

And now, dear one, know that you are in the presence of the Archangels

Feel our love as we extend it to you

And know that we are with you, Always and Forever.

Amen.

Okay!! Geoff Back!! I hope that helped :)
Love ya!
Geoff Thompson
MA. B. Kin, AKC, CSEP-CPT
www.discoveringascension.com

As you can see, this was powerful advice from the Archangel Collective as perceived and interpreted by Geoff. This was huge for me in my understanding and practicing of unconditional love, detachment and acceptance of differences. It became a knowing that we are not supposed to be the same, we are not supposed to want the same things, we are not supposed to have the same dreams and desires, we are simply supposed to follow our own truth and desires, while making time and opportunity to cross the bridge from our own unique road to our partner's, so that we can share in each other's dreams and desires, respecting that they are different and that they are supposed to be different.

It takes courage to venture into this realm and to truly seek your own truth, practicing the Tools of Intention and learning what unconditional love actually is. The tools are there to help us find our truth and alignment, but it is the daily practice, the journey that matters. It is the detachment, the acceptance, and most importantly, the non-judgment that creates the fabulous joy that arises from watching someone we love seek and find their own truth; even when it is very different from our own. It is the ability to truly love someone, knowing that it means you may be apart for a while and that you will need to seek opportunities to cross the bridge and join their journey, even for small moments of time. Because it is your unique journey that matters. It is your journey of seeking your truth and alignment that will bring you the greatest joy, passion and abundance. It is this journey that illuminates the path to how you can serve others while experiencing your true nature. It is also what will allow you to appreciate and accept the unique journey your life partner is on. Remember, we are not supposed to take the same road to a specific destination; we are only supposed to make a commitment to wait for the other person when we get there. We all get there when the time is just right for us.

Bob and I continue to detangle. When we find ourselves in an argument or disagreement we quickly monitor ourselves (Observer). We evaluate the involvement of the Ego and the win/lose mentality and make a different choice. A significant indicator of our progress is how quickly we can now move through these moments. We step back and remember that we are not supposed to agree. It is not only okay to be different, it is essential to the growth and development of our own unique Spiritual Alignment. We quickly remove judgment, and find unconditional love knowing that the other person is supposed to seek their truth, not follow ours.

# CHAPTER TWELVE

# ORGANIZATIONAL LEADERSHIP

**Creating Positive Energy for Leaders**

The Tools of Intention and the practices of Spiritually Aligned Leadership apply not only in our parenting role and intimate relationships, but also in our role as an organizational leader. In fact this is my true passion. Imagine an organization where every manager, supervisor, emerging leader, and executive are working on their Spiritual Alignment while carrying out their duties and responsibilities. Now take it a step further and imagine that every employee within that organization is also Spiritually Aligned. They lead themselves every day, ensuring that the only tree they are nurturing and caring for is their own Tree of Abundance. What would that look and feel like? Now if the organization also has a strong compelling purpose that everyone feels and understands, you have a recipe for amazing impact, profitability, attraction of talent, engagement and the list goes on. If you are still fundamentally rooted in fear, you may think a business environment like this would be chaotic and out of control, but if you are already creating positive energy in your life, you can surely imagine the significant, positive impact this would have on organizational life, productivity, and collaboration, not to mention profitability.

It begins with believing that at the core of each one of us is a person (spirit) that wants to do well, wants to contribute in a positive way, and wants to serve and enhance the life of others and our organizations. I believe that our true nature is to seek our unique source of joy and our passion; through this joy and passion we are able to nurture our spirit while serving others and helping our organizations accomplish amazing results. This may seem to be a very foreign concept to you, or incredibly naive and unrealistic, but I have seen and experienced it and know that it absolutely can and does exist.

I'll begin by exploring our old energy organizations and then we will look at our Spiritually Aligned and positive (newer) energy organizations.

## Old Energy Organizations

An old energy organization requires that employees do what they are told and what they are hired to do, regardless of whether they are happy, fulfilled or in alignment. The organization may say otherwise, but their actions do not. These organizations often wonder why their engagement levels are so low, and they continually try to engage their workforce with new initiatives and programs; all of which produce minimal results. These organizations are trying their best, but because they are out of alignment, their efforts have minimal impact.

Within these old energy organizations you will find leaders who are not honest and open with regard to what they truly feel and think. They are entrenched in the corporate dogma of rules and regulations, and are usually disconnected from their own inner voice, relying only on the left-brain activity with a dash of right-brain and no activation of the heart-center. It is a linear and mechanistic approach to management and leadership. These leaders are often highly stressed and unhappy, working extremely hard and yet feeling they are making little progress. The stress and unhappiness is a direct sign that they are out of alignment; however, they simply think it comes with the territory. *Work isn't supposed to be fun.* The belief is that successful leaders work really hard and stress comes with the territory.

Many of these organizations still operate from a fear-based perspective. They focus primarily on risk management and use extensive rules, policies and procedures to guide every choice and decision. They try to create a rule or policy to cover absolutely every scenario that *might* occur and, as a result, no one makes a decision without checking the rulebook first. If these organizations were truly honest and were willing to answer the hard questions, they would discover that an underlying negative layer of risk avoidance or "what if" scenarios guides many of their decisions. I am not suggesting that organizations should not do detailed analysis and seek out hard evidence and all that is tangible; however, the decision-making criteria should not solely be based on left-brain thinking.

Organizations like this have rigid work environments where managers and employees go along with decisions out of a feeling of fear and/or need to comply with the rules. Creativity is stifled and in some cases non-existent. Everyone is simply *making it work.* Joy is scarce in these organizations and employees would not consider seeking their passion, as this is a foreign concept. *Work is supposed to be hard.*

There is probably a beautiful mission and vision statement hanging in the main hallway of most of these old energy organizations, but when employees are asked, "Do you know what it is? Do you believe it is lived? Do you think there is alignment with it?" Most will respond indifferently or they might respond with a definite *no, no* and *no.*

In many of these organizations, only a small number of individuals at the top of the organization make decisions and everyone else is expected to follow without question. This is how we keep control. This is also how we manage expectations.

We often find, in old energy organizations, a very negative view of our younger generation and the belief that they are frivolous and unfocused. I often hear leaders from these organizations saying that this younger, technically savvy, generation, have no loyalty, no commitment, no social skills, and that they will up and leave at the first sign of not getting their own way. These leaders never consider that perhaps the younger employee does not stay because there is nothing to align to; there is no true compelling reason to work there and the misalignment is so obvious. These young, bright, new employees believe it is possible to love your work and be connected to something bigger and more meaningful than just a paycheck. They want to make a difference and contribute to something important. They want alignment with themselves and their organization.

The age of the *old energy* organization is slowly coming to an end. This is because people who work in these businesses are tired of feeling uninspired, of being underutilized, underappreciated and disempowered. Both young and old alike want autonomy. They want to seek their joy and passion. People are beginning to ask the really hard questions about joy and balance and spiritual awakening. They want relief from the old energy. There is another way.

## Spiritually Aligned Organizations

Spiritually Aligned organizations have, at the core of everything, a compelling purpose. It may or may not be framed and hanging in the hallway. It is, more importantly, lived, talked about and ingrained in every decision. It is the "why we are in business" which has nothing to do with profits. Profits are results, not why we do, what we do. A compelling purpose is simply *who we are*. I write extensively in my first book about what a compelling purpose is and provide a comparison between a *compelling purpose* and the old mission and vision statements. You can also refer to the brief definition in the introduction of this book.

There is no expectation that everyone has to be in full alignment with the compelling purpose; however, if you are not in alignment, then you may choose to leave or be compassionately asked to leave so that you might find an organization with better alignment for you. This happens organically because your Spiritually Aligned Leaders know how to create such an environment with no effort or stress. Sound easy? It is.

We envision organizations that will eventually have Human Resource professionals who specialize in coaching employees who have identified a lack of alignment. Spiritually Aligned organizations will encourage employees to self-identify when they cannot find alignment. These employees are the ones that are under-performing, have high absenteeism and are more prone to illness and stress.

We believe that these employees absolutely know that they are under-performing, out of alignment (they may not use this language) and not feeling well. They are stressed just thinking about work and they dread Monday morning. They may not be honest with themselves, but this is often because our organizations don't provide the right environment for employees to be candid. Honesty is not encouraged or rewarded and therefore the employee is afraid to be honest. In the Spiritually Aligned, new energy organization, this environment is absolutely present at all times. It is the backbone of productivity, attracting the right employees with the right skill sets, and creating an environment where employees, who don't feel they fit and cannot find alignment, can move on comfortably and safely with no negative or punitive ramifications. Alignment is a common word. Managers, leaders and Human Resources assist these employees in an open and transparent fashion.

These employees are coached to be honest with themselves and to identify why they are feeling out of alignment. Sometimes it is a simple case of finding a more suitable role for the employee within the organization, sometimes it is a role misalignment. Sometimes the under-performance is a very temporary situation due to a change in the person's personal life. However, often it is the employee feeling out of alignment with the views, philosophy and culture of the organization. The Human Resources department will assist these employees, with no judgment attached, in finding appropriate alternative employment and will recognize that this is a valued and acceptable practice.

In the USA, it is estimated that disengaged employees are one of the top reasons for lost productivity. These employees suffer for years while the employer pays the price of low productivity. Instead of using the law and courts to govern our actions, why not create a compassionate and Spiritually Aligned Leadership team that encourages and assists under-performing employees to self-identify, ask the hard questions and then prepare for re-assignment either in or outside of the company. Spiritually Aligned organizations create a safe place for employees to be honest with themselves and others. It is not only encouraged it is expected. However, it all starts with the Spiritually Aligned Leader.

In a Spiritually Aligned organization, the leaders find their voices because it is encouraged and valued. They understand the importance and significance of leading-self first and foremost, and that they cannot ever lead others if they are not leading themselves. They are candid and challenge the decisions within the alignment of the compelling purpose every day, and they are also able to accept and detach. They know that these tools are critical to being Spiritually Aligned, and that if they have too many days in a row where they feel out of alignment, they need to ask themselves the hard questions. The *hard questions* include curiosity about why they might be unhappy, feeling uninspired or overly stressed or anxious. Remember that not feeling good is an indication that something isn't right or that something needs to be explored. This exploration is encouraged and in fact expected. The organization is honest about who they are and encourage their contributors to be honest about their fit within that framework.

Recently, I coached a leader in Western Canada who described a situation where the employees within his department were always coming to him to complain about others. He believed in an open door policy and that his team should have access to seeking his advice. As our discussion unfolded, it was apparent that this leader disliked conflict and felt it was his job to assist team members in getting along. He was also trying to create harmony and to mediate differences. He believed this was one of his responsibilities, however he didn't enjoy it and was feeling burdened by all of the time demands being made on him by his staff. It was not a positive environment. He talked about how difficult it was, as individuals continually came to him with issues of other people's performance. He described the office as becoming a soap opera.

My client gave an example of a situation where Sally (one of his team members) had come to him with a concern regarding the quality of Joshua's work. Some important documents were not completed correctly. My client described how he advised Sally that he would look into it and would speak with Joshua. I asked my client what message Sally might have gotten from this discussion. As he reflected and explored, this he determined that the message was, *It's okay to bring me your problems, I will look after everything. It's okay to talk negatively about another employee or even to rat them out for poor quality of work.* This leader wanted to solve everyone else's issues, smooth the waters. This was his natural preference, but in doing so, he had created an environment where he was seen as the go-to-person for every issue. Staff were disempowered and had been trained (sub-consciously) to seek his advice on everything. In our coaching I asked him how could he be an intentional and deliberate leader; how could he adjust his style to meet the needs of this situation and get a different result? As he asked himself the hard questions, the leader had a light-bulb moment, looked me in the eye and said, "I think I may have created this situation." He came to realize that he needed to change his approach (lead-self) and that others would discover the value of leading themselves through his example.

He started to ask each employee that came to his office some simple questions. Some of the examples he came up with during our discussion were to ask Sally the following:

► How does what Joshua did affect you being able to do your job?

► Have you spoken directly to Joshua about your concern?    ·

► How could you assist Joshua?

A simple change in approach has a completely different result. By asking these questions what message would Sally get? Maybe the message for Sally is, *Joshua's poor performance is not affecting me, why would I bring this to my boss. It appears like my boss thinks I could handle this myself, maybe I should speak with Joshua. Maybe I could help him.* Through this discussion, the leader was now setting an example of Leading-Self and was clearly expecting Sally to do the same. He can have a coaching conversation with Sally that allows Sally to work through the issues.

His goal was to have Sally recognize that she was very capable of seeking her own answers and finding ways to interact positively with others. As he began to ask his team questions, they began to believe their leader truly thought they could solve their own issues. The new message was, *I trust you and know that you have the knowledge and skill to navigate your interpersonal relationships in a positive way.* This is a very simple example of how when a leader turns inward and asks, *What am I doing to create this situation and what can I do to lead-self.* A completely different result can be realized. The leader does not need to tell his employees, "Don't come to my office with your complaints." The leader needs to believe that all individuals have the answers and are capable of leading-self and that the leader's role is to create the right environment and set an example.

For the organization to be highly productive, it must also have happy, aligned employees who absolutely enjoy what they are doing and know that their work is meaningful. High productivity is a result of empowered individuals who are connected to the organization's compelling purpose, to their work (tasks) and to each other. Remember that at the core of these organizations is positive energy based on Spiritual Alignment and a knowing that each person truly wants to do well, belong, contribute and serve in a meaningful way. The leaders create this environment through their own *self-leadership* and by practicing the Tools of Intention

In our leadership courses one of our core lessons is; *Leadership has everything to do with the leader and nothing to do with the leader all at the same time.* This means that the leader clearly understands that they must be self-centered, lead-self from the inside out (*all about them*), do the hard work so that they can set an example and create organic influence. This does not mean that they agree with every decision made in the organization. These leaders apply the tools of acceptance, detachment and non-judgment. They recognize that it is not about getting one's own way all of the time, but it is about contributing and accepting while monitoring the internal conversations. If a decision is contrary to their personal approach, the leader may ask themselves: Why does this bother me? Can I accept and let go and support this decision? Is the decision still in alignment with our compelling purpose and values? Often a leader will realize that it is simply the Ego playing its role, at which time the leader can observe what is happening and choose another approach. They choose better thoughts, feelings and behaviors and immediately get relief and better results.

We have coached hundreds of leaders and many of them arrive feeling frustrated, overworked and unhappy. Our role is to encourage the leader to begin by being honest with him or herself.

Once they begin to do this, they often discover how out of alignment they are with their beliefs, values, skill set and overall passions. As the leader begins to explore this, they open themselves up to discovering their true self and there is an immediate sense of relief. This relief comes with some fear, but also with significant joy. Over time some of our clients make the decision to follow their newly uncovered passions and they begin to look for an organization where there is better alignment. It is a process not a destination and as long as the client is accepting of their situation, detached from any rigid expectations of the future, clear on their desires and passions (joy), they can slowly move forward monitoring their thoughts and creating good feelings which will ultimately result in a great shift.

## A Personal Story

I started my business in 2002 and by 2012 it had grown significantly. We had thirteen full-time consultants and trainers and were working in all areas of Human Resources. However, something wasn't right. I felt unfulfilled, frustrated and tired. I had been feeling this way for some time, but had been reluctant to be honest. I can still remember very clearly the catalyst that shifted me. I made a trip to New York and had the opportunity to briefly meet with Cheryl Richardson, a master coach and best-selling author. I shared my frustrations with her and before I knew it she had coached me exactly the way I often work with my clients. She simply said, "Close your eyes and keep them closed, now go deep inside, you know the truth, you have the answers, you are just avoiding being honest with yourself." I was quickly reminded that I had not been the intentional and deliberate self-leader that I believed so strongly in. I was not being an Observer or tapping into my truth. In fact, I was avoiding my truth for many reasons. The truth was I never really wanted to be a business owner, managing contracts and other consultants. I wanted to coach, write, teach and public speak. I was a consultant not a manager. That was my truth! However, over time, the business had grown and in many ways did not resemble what I truly wanted. I was bogged down in administration, unfulfilling work and daily management. On the surface, others would see a successful business owner who had it all, but, nothing could be further from the truth. I was unhappy. I started to really ask myself, *What do I truly want? How would I feel if I was out from underneath this significant responsibility?* I began to make the very tough personal decisions. Some might see this as selfish, but it wasn't because my team had known for some time that I was not happy. We can't hide from those around us. We take our energy with us everywhere we go.

Slowly I decided to downsize, restructure and purge everything that did not bring me joy. The following eighteen months were full of tough yet important and aligned decision-making. Contracts weren't renewed, some employees were respectfully transitioned to new employment, we moved out of our large office space, assets were sold, a portion of the business was sold and much of it was given away to other consulting firms. It was an eighteen-month roller coaster ride of lawyers, accountants and periods of great fear. I was becoming self-centered, truly focusing on what *I* was meant to do, re-aligning the company's compelling purpose and getting back on track with my joy, passion and truth.

It is very important to also note that I was detached and accepting of what would come. I had to let go and know that trying to control or plan every step was not only impossible, but also unproductive. I had to accept things as they came and put one foot in front of the other, even when there were moments of incredible fear. I would ask myself, every morning for eighteen months, *Am I moving in the direction of my truth?* and if so, I would observe my Roommate, manage my thoughts and monitor how I felt every day. I consciously chose good feeling thoughts and each day I imagined what it would feel like to be on the other side, only doing what I loved. This may sound like it was not that big a deal, but when you have hired every employee, trained and worked with them, it was extremely tough to re-align and make different choices. It was hard on those let go, hard on those that stayed and was difficult for several clients who did not necessarily fully understand my choices. However, in the end, everyone landed incredibly well and looked back saying, that it was not only the right thing, but was necessary.

The result was amazing. As we began to purge, we made room for the work that I truly wanted to do. I felt relief and a new sense of energy and passion. Our Leadership Programming and Customization was growing quickly and I was now doing work every day that I was passionate about. We had moved from twelve full-time consultants and 3000 square feet of office including a small training center to two trainers/coaches and one 200 square foot office. We had said goodbye to several hundred thousand dollars' worth of contracts. Nothing looked the same. We were aligned, focused and I was overjoyed with the end result.

When individual contributors are encouraged to be honest about their own desires and intentions, because their employer truly wants them to find their personal joy and passion, amazing things happen. The leader encourages them to align with the corporate compelling purpose or move to an organization or career where they can align. Imagine every employee practicing the Tools of Intention while remaining firmly on their own tree focused on their own journey (productivity). They monitor their

Ego and fears and replace them with positive thoughts, feelings and behaviors. Each employee learns to accept and detach and knows that boulder pushing is energy-sucking and a waste of time. However, at the same time, they know that if they are unhappy for any length of time, that they are responsible for going inside, doing the right evaluation and making new decisions that will move them forward. Those decisions will either be in alignment with the corporation or not and that is completely okay. Imagine the productivity that can occur when an entire group of people are Spiritually Aligned knowing that they are contributing to a compelling purpose that matters.

This is the way of the future. It will not be isolated and only available to a select few employees in a select few companies. Companies with old energy will go through significant transitions on their journey to Creating Positive Energy, but they will have no choice as employees become more and more discerning, clear on what they want and focused on their own desires, intentions and alignment.

# CHAPTER THIRTEEN

# CLOSING THOUGHTS

I believe that the culture we have been living in for the past 100 years is over and that we are on a new journey of self-discovery, where individuals will truly begin to learn about their personal powers to create anything they want.

Parents and children alike will become the catalysts for change within our homes and school systems. This is inevitable. Parents will challenge the status quo and begin to allow their children to follow the beat of their own drum from conception to adulthood with no extraneous expectations or value judgments about what is right and what is wrong. Parents will encourage their children to seek their own truth, joy and passions and there will be a clear understanding that when a person is following their joy, they will ultimately find a way to serve others through that joy. Parents will stop believing that their children are born as a blank slate requiring a teacher for everything, but will trust their children and their children's inner voice. Parents will understand the difference between being selfish and being self-centered. Acceptance and detachment will become the norm as parents and children crave free-flowing unconditional love.

As these amazing young people emerge into the workforce,

leaders will be prepared to engage and expand their own views of leadership. They will understand that everything begins with them and them alone. They are not there to tell others what to do, but to lead the way by example, and to show each and every employee the joy and bliss that comes from being Spiritually Aligned. These leaders recognize their responsibility to create positive energy and to live by example, sharing a road map to happiness and joy. They pride themselves on living their core values of *honesty before kindness that comes from good intentions.* Their honesty with another person is not based on a negative judgment resulting in making the other person wrong, but is based on the good intention of assisting another person in seeking their own truth. They are not afraid to be candid with someone about what they sense and feel about a situation and encourage others to do the same. However, they would never be so bold as to think they have the answers for another person. They do not judge or have negative feelings toward anyone or any situation although they may disagree. Spiritually Aligned Leaders do this after thorough reflection and consideration. They are true Observers of their thoughts, feelings and behaviors and are quick to correct alignment whenever they see derailment occurring. They consciously and deliberately use acceptance and detachment to assist them in monitoring and removing judgment and Ego. They don't have to win.

Businesses will flourish, but under a completely different set of paradigms. Leadership will flow throughout the corporation where employees are making great decisions because of a love and respect for the company and a belief in its values and goals. Successful corporations will have a compelling purpose that employees want to align with and those organizations will attract the right people for the right reasons. Employees will not be angry when things do not go their way, as they will understand that they live in a world of free will and that they can choose a new path any time, for any reason. They simply have to address their fears, let go of the victim mentality, remove their judgments and take right action for themselves. They have the inner power and most importantly they have a heart-center that will speak to them if only they learn to truly listen and act on it.

Becoming a Spiritually Aligned Leader is a journey that never ends and practicing the Tools of Intention requires commitment, focus and a belief that we can receive and experience significant relief. The relief eventually shifts to acceptance and then to balance and peace. Eventually, as we practice the tools over and over again, our energy shifts to one of joy and seeking our passion. Once we discover our passion, it is through following this passion that we serve the larger community. If we allow ourselves to believe that we are deserving and worthy, that we can have abundance and that joy and passion are our birthright, then we can create positive energy everywhere we go. The right road will reveal itself to us. Our tree will grow a new branch that shows us the way. We do not need to push boulders or be a victim. We simply need to believe that we are worthy. As you nurture your Tree of Abundance remember your role is to care for and practice the Tools of Intention, to be self-centered so that you can truly be a Spiritually Aligned Leader with immense organic influence.

Lead Yourself and the Rest Will Follow

# EPILOGUE

Two weeks after the first draft of the book was finished, my father passed away.

## Divine Order and Co-Creation

Our world works in glorious synchronicity when we slow down, practice being intentional, deliberate and Spiritually Aligned. The week that my dad was hospitalized, Geoff, Mike (two sons who live in Central Canada) and I were heading west (Victoria, BC) for some work with a new client. I had originally intended to be in Winnipeg for a gala awards dinner, but decided at the last minute that I could not turn down the opportunity that presented itself with this new client. I made the difficult decision to not attend the awards gala, and headed to Victoria with some of my colleagues (who also happen to be my sons).

At the same time, I had a client in Winnipeg who changed their training dates, so I was able to jump an earlier flight thinking that I would spend some time with my husband for a couple of days prior to our Victoria event.

In beautiful order, the morning I arrived in Victoria was the morning my father was hospitalized. My father did not know I was coming. There is no family that live close that would visit him, but here I was at the Victoria airport when I received a call from the homecare staff to say that he was at the hospital. My husband had picked me up at the airport, so off we went to see my dad. He has been hospitalized many times, so we thought it was just another setback.

It was apparent from the moment we saw him, that this was different. I was able to spend the next five days with my dad, traveling back and forth from my home on the Gulf Islands to the hospital. Over those five days my dad moved from highly cognitive to delusional and being unaware of where he was. On one of his good days we were chatting about birthdays and age. My dad had recently turned eighty-six years old. In beautiful and true form for my dad, he said, "I know that I am in palliative care and that I am supposed to die, but your mom lived three and half months after her eighty-sixth birthday and I want to do the same. I want to live longer than your mom did." I said to him, "Dad you have to be kidding me. Is it truly a competition," he laughed and said, "Absolutely, it's a competition."

A couple of days later, Geoff and Mike arrived as planned. Here I was on the west coast with my entire family (which has never happened). My middle son, Scott, lives in Victoria. I have wanted to have everyone together for years, but it just didn't work out, but at the exact moment my dad was hospitalized for the last time, we were all together; able to say good-bye to someone who had a significant impact on us all.

Some of you would say, "Just a coincidence" I would say, "Divine Order". Intentional practice of Spiritually Aligned Leadership assists us in co-creating the exact world we want.

### Reflect, Reconnect, Renew

My dad had a profound impact on all of his six children for many different reasons. We have not been a close family and are spread across Canada, as well as one sister who lives in Australia. A death creates a unique environment for reflection, reconnection and renewal. This is how I choose to see the death of my dad.

My dad is one of the reasons I believe we have not been a close family. He created a very competitive environment and although his intentions were good, the results were not. A sense of winning has plagued our relationships and a focus on getting my dad's love and attention made it sometimes adversarial.

As we prepared to come together to mourn our loss and celebrate a life, I wondered how it would all go. I was optimistic and open to every opportunity and was looking forward to seeing everyone.

These are major events in a person's life and sometimes they can bring back some not so great memories. Not this time. Every memory was a pleasing one. We talked about how playful dad was and how he loved to read to us when we were little. We talked about how he had a love of nature and being outside and how taking a long walk was one of the most thought provoking activities we did as a family. I reconnected with my siblings in a way I have not done for decades.

I expected heaviness, but in fact there was a lighthearted and renewed sense of life and purpose. There is nothing to read into this, and no judgments, just a true celebration of a life. My dad was what tied us together, but was also part of why we were driven apart. Today my dad is a catalyst for renewal and rejuvenation. One of the themes for me was a renewed confirmation that unconditional love is not only possible, but easy when a person removes judgments and expectations and is simply open and accepting.

I am grateful for all of the roles my dad played both in life and after death.

Creating the life you have always wanted full of passion, joy and abundance is right around the corner. Relief from the day-to-day three dimensional dramas is available to all of us. Rewarding careers, fabulous health, spontaneous serendipity, joy and passion for life *is* possible.

## ENVIRONMENTAL BENEFITS STATEMENT

**Change Innovators** saved the following resources by printing the pages of this book on chlorine free paper made with 100% post-consumer waste.

| TREES | WATER | ENERGY | SOLID WASTE | GREENHOUSE GASES |
|---|---|---|---|---|
| 8 | 3,770 | 4 | 253 | 695 |
| FULLY GROWN | GALLONS | MILLION BTUs | POUNDS | POUNDS |

Environmental impact estimates were made using the Environmental Paper Network Paper Calculator3.2. For more information visit www.papercalculator.org.